MANAGING INTERNATIONAL STUDENTS

Managing Universities and Colleges:
Guides to Good Practice

Series editors:

David Warner, Principal and Chief Executive, Swansea Institute of Higher Education

David Palfreyman, Bursar and Fellow, New College, Oxford

This series has been commissioned in order to provide reference manuals of good practice on the major areas of the management of colleges and universities.

Current titles
John M. Gledhill: *Managing Students*
Christine Humfrey: *Managing International Students*
Colleen Liston: *Managing Quality and Standards*

Forthcoming titles include
Allan Bolton: *Managing the Academic Unit*
Ann Edworthy: *Managing Stress*
Judith Elkin and Derek Law (eds): *Managing Information*
David Nicol: *Managing Learning and Teaching*
Andrew Paine: *Managing Hospitality Services*
Harold Thomas: *Managing Financial Resources*
David Watson: *Managing Strategy*

MANAGING INTERNATIONAL STUDENTS

Recruitment to graduation

Christine Humfrey

Open University Press
Buckingham · Philadelphia

Open University Press
Celtic Court
22 Ballmoor
Buckingham
MK18 1XW

e-mail: enquiries@openup.co.uk
world wide web: http://www.openup.co.uk

and
325 Chestnut Street
Philadelphia, PA 19106, USA

First Published 1999

A catalogue record of this book is available from the British Library

ISBN   0 335 20308 6 (hb)   0 335 20307 8 (pb)

Library of Congress Cataloging-in-Publication Data
Humfrey, Christine, 1947–
   Managing international students:recruitment to graduation /
Christine Humfrey.
      p.   cm. – (Managing colleges and universities)
   Includes bibliographical references (p.   ) and index.
   ISBN 0-335-20308-6 (hard). – ISBN 0-335-20307-8 (pbk.)
   1. Students, Foreign–Great Britain.   2. College students–
Recruiting–Great Britain.   3. International education–Great
Britain.   I. Title.   II. Series.
LB2376.6.G7H86   1997
378. 1'9826'91–DC21
                                                    99-17597
                                                       CIP

Typeset by Graphicraft Limited, Hong Kong
Printed in Great Britain by The Cromwell Press, Trowbridge

For our international students who trust us with their dreams – and for Michael, to whom I entrust mine.

CONTENTS

SERIES EDITORS' INTRODUCTION

Post-secondary educational institutions can be viewed from a variety of different perspectives. For the majority of students and staff who work in them, they are centres of learning and teaching where the participants are there by choice and consequently, by and large, work very hard. Research has always been important in some higher education institutions, but in recent years this emphasis has grown and what for many was a great pleasure and, indeed, a treat is becoming more of a threat and an insatiable performance indicator which just has to be met. Maintaining the correct balance between quality research and learning/teaching, while the unit of resource continues to decline inexorably, is one of the key issues facing us all. Educational institutions as work places must be positive and not negative environments.

From another aspect, post-secondary educational institutions are clearly communities, functioning to all intents and purposes like small towns and internally requiring and providing a similar range of services, while also having very specialist needs. From yet another, they are seen as external suppliers of services to industry, commerce and the professions. These 'customers' receive, *inter alia*, a continuing flow of well-qualified fresh graduates with transferable skills; part-time and short course study opportunities through which to develop existing employees; consultancy services to solve problems and help expand business; and research and development support to create new breakthroughs.

However, educational institutions are also significant businesses in their own right. One recent study of the economic impact of higher education in Wales shows that it is of similar importance in employment terms to the steel or banking/finance sectors. Put another way, Welsh higher education institutions (HEIs) spend half a billion pounds annually and create more than 23,000 full-time equivalent jobs. And it must be remembered that there are only 13 HEIs in Wales, compared with 175 in the whole of the UK, and that these Welsh institutions are, on average, relatively small. In addition, it has recently been realized that UK higher education is a major export industry with the added benefit of long-term financial and political returns. If the UK further education sector is also added to this equation, then the economic impact of post-secondary education is of truly startling proportions.

Whatever perspective you take, it is obvious that educational institutions require managing and, consequently, this series has been produced to facilitate that end. The editors have striven to identify authors who are distinguished practitioners in their own right and can also write. The authors have been given the challenge of producing essentially practical handbooks which combine appropriate theory and contextual material with many examples of good practice and guidance.

The topics chosen are of key importance to educational management and stand at the forefront of current debate. Some of these topics have never been covered in depth before and all of them are equally applicable to further as well as higher education. The editors are firmly of the belief that the UK distinction between these sectors will continue to blur and will be replaced, as in many other countries, by a continuum where the management issues are entirely common.

For well over a decade, both of the editors have been involved with a management development programme for senior staff from higher education institutions throughout the world. Every year the participants quickly learn that we share the same problems and that similar solutions are normally applicable. Political and cultural differences may on occasion be important, but are often no more than an overlying veneer. Hence, this series will be of considerable relevance and value to post-secondary educational managers in many countries.

We mentioned earlier that UK higher education has become a major export industry. This has been achieved by its international work, primarily involving the recruitment of full-cost fee-paying students to UK-based courses, but more recently through the growing provision of franchised and validated programmes overseas. This third volume in the series deals thoroughly with the subject of international students and, most appropriately, is subtitled 'Recruitment to Graduation' because this is the virtuous circle which must be completed perfectly in order to remain in business.

Christine Humfrey has worked for a long time on the international scene and this shows throughout the book. There are countless examples of good practice and advice, which can only have been gained by personal (and sometimes painful) experience. Nevertheless, the book also displays considerable scholarship, particularly in the first chapter which meticulously traces the history of the current UK situation. There has been much fragmented writing on this subject, but at last it has been drawn together into a comprehensive and very valuable account.

David Warner
David Palfreyman

PREFACE

International education, in what has been described as its 'classical' form, encompasses the freedom objectively to evaluate ideas from whatever nation or culture they come; the enrichment of case studies by examples drawn from outside the host system; the recognition of qualifications from other education systems; the support for student integration at whatever level of entry their intellect and attainment allows; the sharing of discovery in collaborative research; the willingness to include new perspectives in the curriculum; the enthusiasm for travel to other institutions and the encouragement of that energy and excitement in students and teachers; the willingness to recognize the worth of other institutions. At its highest level, the benefits of such education could be global understanding and harmony – more realistically, they should at least include the facilitation of friendships across international boundaries, more effective development of the global knowledge base and more interesting programmes for students at every level.

International education is not limited to the higher education sector, although it can be most obviously displayed there and possibly most easily resourced. It can occur in the primary school, when the children of international visitors are welcomed to the classroom. It can take place in the class preparing for secondary school examinations, and in all sectors of secondary education. Further education can provide an opportunity for home and overseas students to work together, in access and academic programmes, in vocational courses, and in specialist skill training.

The concept of international education does not belong to Britain, nor to Europe, but to every country whose scholars wish to extend their intellectual horizons. It belongs to those who leave their countries to obtain it, as much as to those who open their doors to such visitors to offer it. 'Home' as well as 'overseas' students should all benefit by the interaction. International education is not new. Education by its very definition must promote an international awareness – without that awareness, those who teach and learn cannot understand the context into which knowledge fits. Without context it is difficult for knowledge to become wisdom, or for the clever student to become the educated adult.

The 'classical' concept of international education in Europe included the medieval migration of scholars, the broadening of the history curriculum offered in schools, the participation in the post-Second World War European student mobility schemes, such as ERASMUS and SOCRATES. Such schemes have been extended into Eastern Europe with TEMPUS and other programmes. These, however, are the background to and not the subject of this book. As Chapter 1 will show, this classical view of international education was changed by the events of the late 1970s and early 1980s across the world. When the governments of many of the developed nations decided to restrict entry to their higher education systems, the institutions themselves responded by developing a new policy, new skills, new literature and, indeed, a new profession – that of international student recruitment and care. This book focuses on these developments. While every institution will quite honestly, in most cases, claim that one of its objectives is international education in the classical sense, it will also be very obvious that 'international' will mean income generating and will be prioritized accordingly. The drive to recruit this type of international student which began in the higher education institutions in the 1980s had an impact on further education, the school sector and the language schools and colleges. Certain basic marketing and management skills had to be learned, regardless of the type of institution. Any institution which aspired to be a key player in the international field was suddenly obliged to undertake planning, resourcing and implementation for the new task. Of course, the drive to recruit this type of international student was not limited to the United Kingdom (UK). Australia, New Zealand, North America, Germany, France and, more recently, centres in Asia all wanted to recruit appropriate overseas students. Planning to attract, assess and accommodate the bright intellect from overseas is an issue of common concern.

While this book is rooted in the circumstance of higher education in the UK, it seeks to offer ideas which can be taken up widely across the sectors within the UK and appropriately by those overseas institutions whom we have ruefully come to cherish as competitors as well as colleagues.

To this end, and to facilitate the international reader's understanding of some specific UK procedures and vocabulary, a glossary of acronyms and abbreviations is provided.

ACKNOWLEDGEMENTS

It might be argued that educational management and international relations are two of the more interesting areas for employment and study. To be able to work in a capacity that spans them both is a privilege – to be allowed to write about them is a real pleasure.

Writing a book such as this is an invitation to describe best practice and to set it in a conceptual and developmental context. If such a book is written by a practitioner, the reader might be tempted to assume that what is advocated is what the writer has achieved – if only this were always the case! I have learned a great deal during the preparation of the book.

Now it is leaving my hands I would like to thank the British Council for providing access with help and hospitality to their archive Board and Committee minutes, Desmond Lauder for recalling his early memories of the Education Counselling Service, Dr White at the Cripps Health Centre, the University of Nottingham, for checking the validity of the healthcare section of Chapter 4, my editor who made me believe that writing this could be fun, and then ensured that it was, and Nicola May who, with this as with so many other aspects of my office life, created order with hard work and good humour. I am fortunate, too, in having a husband whose interest in the project is only exceeded by his patience in proof reading it! Family and friends offered unstinting encouragement and support, as they have through so many other endeavours.

Colleagues in this country and overseas have contributed so much both in experiences shared and knowledge passed on. The views expressed here are enriched by their wisdom and companionship.

ABBREVIATIONS

A Level	Advanced level
ACU	Association of Commonwealth Universities
APA	Association of Polytechnic Administrators
APT	Advanced Placement Test
CICHE	Committee for International Co-operation in Higher Education
CONACYT	Consejo Nacional de Ciencia y Tecnologia
CUA	Conference of University Administrators
CVCP	Committee of Vice Chancellors and Principals
DTI	Department of Trade and Industry
ECS	Education Counselling Service
ERASMUS	The European Community Action Scheme for the Mobility of University Students
FCO	Foreign and Commonwealth Office
FEFC	Further Education Funding Council
GCSE	General Certificate of Secondary Education
GPA	Grade Point Average
GP	General Practitioner
HEFC	Higher Education Funding Council
HEQC	Higher Education Quality Council
HEU (students)	Home and European Union (students)
HOST	Hospitality for Overseas Students Trust
IB	International Baccalaureate
IELTS	International English Language Testing Service
KCSE	Kenyan Certificate of Secondary Education
LSE	London School of Economics
MASN	Maximum Aggregate Student Number
MRes	Master of Research

NARIC	The National Academic Recognition Information Centre (NARIC) for the United Kingdom
NCIHE	National Committee of Inquiry into Higher Education
NHS	National Health Service
ODASS	Overseas Development Agency Scholarship Scheme
ORS	Overseas Research Students Scheme
RAE	Research Assessment Exercise
SAT	Scholastic Aptitude Test
SSR	Staff–student Ratio
STPM	Sijil Tinggi Persekolahan Malaysia
TOEFL	Test of English as a Foreign Language
UCAS	Universities Central Admissions Service
UGC	University Grants Committee
UKCOSA	United Kingdom Council for Overseas Student Affairs
YÖK	The Higher Education Council in Turkey

1

THE WAY WE WERE: A HISTORY OF THE INTERNATIONAL STUDENT

Introduction

The changes which took place in the late 1970s that so dramatically affected international student recruitment to the UK universities are now part of the history of this sector of British education. A true understanding of the impact on the universities of government dictum of this kind can best be achieved by a recognition of the developing relationship between universities and the State, between autonomy and accountability and between the conflicting pressures of public service and the entrepreneurial culture. A review of the method by which the university system was begun, developed and expanded in the United Kingdom can provide a clearer insight into the difficulties which the universities found and into the factors which affected their response.

The UK has one of the oldest traditions of university education in the world and consequently the richness or the 'baggage' of this history could be argued to bring both value and inhibition to the debate.

Education and influence, education and prosperity, education and income have never been seen as mutually exclusive. It may once have been the case that the wandering scholar sat at the feet of Aquinas without thought for tuition fee, but that 'golden' period was short-lived. It should be remembered, too, that in those days the idealistic young people in search of learning were far more likely to be the sons of the affluent classes than those of the agricultural labourer or the artisan. The opportunity of a liberal education, and time to spend in study, was a privilege of those whose family had the means to allow it.

When the medieval *studium generale*[1] moved from communities of interested scholars to something more permanent, it did so through endowments and benefactions. The student following the itinerant scholars across Europe was 'like a Crusader, a pilgrim travelling light and travelling often in quest of the Holy Grail of knowledge' (Fisher 1936). Later, wealthy patrons and their donations undeniably placed some constraints on these students and their embryonic institutions. Gradually, the freedom from things temporal, which was the hallmark of the early institution, was replaced by the questionable, but necessary, benefits of patronage. 'The age of apostolic poverty was succeeded by the age of lavish endowment' (ibid.). Rashdall,[2] writing in 1936 before the age of endowment had completely given way to the age of State support, had believed that the strength of these early institutions had sprung from their poverty. Institutions today are more likely to believe that the ability to generate income – and so attain financial security – must go hand in hand with academic achievement.

Financing the UK higher education system

Poverty, philanthropy and State support 1100–1889

The age of philanthropy and of municipal pioneering endeavour in higher education (HE) was succeeded by that of State aid. Before this happened, Oxford and Cambridge were reformed, London and Durham were established and, finally, the Civic University Movement was successful in creating the breadth of higher educational provision in England, which continued until the Robbins[3] Report of the early 1960s expanded it yet further (Robbins 1963). The Civic Universities and University Colleges established in the nineteenth century were not the creation of the State. Instead, they were a response to the needs of a successful, commercial and manufacturing society, and of communities hungry for enlightenment and intellectual progress. Their objectives were facilitated by individual benefactions or local patriotism. Building upon the extended franchise, improved school provision and the efforts, among others, of the Chartists, the Christian Scientists, the parliamentary Labour Party, the Fabians, the Mechanists' Institutes, the artisans' libraries, the People's Colleges, the Co-operative Societies, the Workers' Education Association and the university extension movement, centres of learning evolved at 11 locations in England between 1850 and 1892. Southampton,

Manchester, Exeter, Newcastle, Leeds, Bristol, Birmingham, Sheffield, Nottingham, Liverpool and Reading all possessed a University College by the end of the nineteenth century.[4] They were in part to respond to the demand for trained and educated manpower from industries based locally, such as metallurgy, textile technology, marine and electric power engineering, pharmacy and agriculture.

This movement was not an example of centralized national planning. It was not State initiated. The freedom from undue political or religious influence of these institutions reflected their accommodation within society, yet independence of the State. *Ad hoc* growth resulted in random provision. Above all, their independence led to uncertainty of survival and financial vulnerability. Reluctantly and hesitantly the State, by its first tiny grant to universities and university colleges in 1889, supported these institutions whose birth it had not planned, and committed itself to rearing them. University education was thus proclaimed as in part the responsibility of the State. The history of the system from 1889 to the report of the Croham Committee of 1987, which reformulated and redirected the UGC (University Grants Committee), is the history of the State and the universities identifying, agreeing and reshaping their role *vis-à-vis* one another. Since the function of neither the State nor the universities is static and since the perception of citizens, taxpayers and scholars is dynamic, the relationship between the two is subject to constant negotiation. A modern complex industrial society has vocational and manpower needs. A sophisticated system of higher education, developed within a liberal environment, committed to freedom of expression, also has needs if it is to fulfil successfully the objectives to which it is dedicated in its charters. The arguments for the autonomy of the university are interesting, if somewhat academic, in a period of economic growth. These same arguments are critical in a period of recession and consequent reduction in public spending.

The growth of State support 1889–1960s

The debate began with the beginning of State support. This support from the taxpayer through the politicians was not provided entirely out of altruism. It was recognized at an early stage that the country's prosperity depended in some part on its educated labour force. As early as 1887 Sir John Lubbock, advancing financial support for the institutions, stated, 'The claims of these colleges were not based alone on their service to learning and study; they were calculated to contribute largely to the material prosperity of the country – our ignorance costs us very much more than our education.'[5] The civic university movement in England was one in which the regions, the philanthropists, the enlightened pioneers and the institutions could take pride. In general, men of vision, enthusiasm and dedication worked to develop individual colleges for the benefit of the citizens and of the locality, contriving that the needs of the industrialist and the aspirations of those registering for courses might be accommodated together within an institution of post-school education.

The UGC, established in 1919, began the formalized financing of higher education through the taxation system. It did so at the end of the First World War and after informed debate on the future of higher education. It recognized the principles upon which State assistance to higher education was based. It was accepted that education could be provided by public funding, by private funding or by a mixed economy, that is, by a judicious combination of the two. The method of provision was a matter of policy, determined by the government on the will of the electorate. Private funding had always existed, including not merely benefactions and patronage external to students but also their own resources and those of their families. Where education is funded privately, to meet private demand, it is argued that it is the assumption that the 'returns' from education are enjoyed primarily and possibly exclusively by the individual being educated.[6] Thereby the student would expect to gain income, status, better conditions of service and enrichment of outlook, all of which accrue to him or her alone. Where, on the other hand, education is funded entirely from the public purse, it is on the assumption that the returns to society are considerably greater than to the individual. This would involve a high level of manpower planning, State intervention and direction of study and employment.

In Britain, the mixed economy in higher education has been adopted as the response to both public need and private demand. Here, in the post-compulsory sphere, it is recognized that both the individual and the State gain from extended educational opportunities.

Even at the early stages the UGC was not a sole contributor to university finances. Parliamentary grants were responsible for one third of the annual income of the universities; roughly another third accrued from fees and examination income and the remaining third from endowments, donations, local authority grants and a miscellany of lesser accounts. The balance remained approximately the same until just before the Second World War when the figures indicate that the support from central government was beginning to increase. By the arrival of peace in 1945 the sharp decline in private philanthropy was marked, the reduction in the local education authority (LEA) contribution was evident and the unrealistic level of the tuition fee

was obvious. It was from 1946 onwards that the increasing depend-
ence of the universities on central government funding was apparent. Indeed, the report of the UGC in 1948 stated 'that the expansion
and improvement of facilities for university education, which the
public interest demanded, could be achieved only with the aid of
largely increased subventions from the Exchequer'.[7] Nearly 70 per
cent of university income was now provided by the taxpayer.

The reduction of State support 1970s and after

The size and proportion of the support for the university system
from the State continued to grow well into the 1960s. In the years
that followed the Robbins explosion, the higher education system
had to survive the movement of the UGC from the Treasury to the
Department of Education and Science; the change in the UGC con-
stitution to that of the Universities Funding Council; the polytechnics and colleges of higher education claiming and receiving a
share of higher education provision and resourcing; the Comptroller
and Auditor General being given access to university financial records;
student unrest; graduate unemployment and the consequent under-
mining of national belief in the value of higher education, both for
itself and for its contribution to the gross domestic product. All
these factors combined with a perceived arrogance on the part
of the universities, and an inability to present themselves to the
public which funded an increasing percentage of their activities. This
occurred at a time of recession throughout industrial society and
a planned campaign to reduce public expenditure, together with a
growing interest in organization and methods, management information and advanced technology. Value for money; appraisal; effectiveness; efficiency; accountability; quality and selectivity; and the
investigation of structures, procedures, standards and governance
were the motivation for such reports as that of Jarratt and Sizer
(1987), and were of themselves laudable objectives. Of these, the
campaign to reduce public expenditure was the most significant for
this book as it led to the establishment of the function of 'marketing' for international students. In 1979 the government changed
from Labour to Conservative. Until this time it had been believed
that the universities had enjoyed what Kogan has described as

> a love affair with Whitehall and Westminster. They (the univer-
> sities) were seen as a glowing example of how government could
> both fund, and keep its hands off, institutions of proven worth,
> and were part of the fabric of the kind of society which many

Conservatives cherished. Here the young could learn to be both independent and yet dependable.

(Kogan 1983)

The new Cabinet was, however, committed to a general reduction of public expenditure.

The overseas fee

In the November 1979 White Paper, universities were faced with a menu of implications which caused confusion and anxiety. The *Times Higher Education Supplement* of November 1979 stated,

> They (the universities) have been both stunned and confused by the government's action; stunned by the nature, intensity and timing of the cuts, and particularly in relation to overseas students, and confused because they still do not have hard figures or prospective student targets with which to work.

At a time when public expenditure on higher education had to be capped, the government looked around for areas in which to retrench. The subsidy on the education of overseas students had to be stopped and a realistic fee for them introduced. The increase of the overseas student fee to the full cost was confirmed. The taxpayer would no longer be helping to provide the higher education of students whose homes were outside the EEC. Ralf Dahrendorf, Director of the London School of Economics (LSE), commented when discussing the imposed overseas fee,

> Our students say the present fee is already beyond their means. We will have to look carefully at all applications. I say this with tears in my eyes; there will definitely be a lowering of standards. We will have to accept some people who have money and not the quality.

(Kogan 1983)

For the government, Dr Rhodes Boyson indicated that overseas students were 'costing' a hundred million pounds a year in fee subsidy. He stated in his *THES* interview,

> All the groans have come from the university lobbies and not from the general populace. Two out of five overseas students are from Iran and Nigeria. We do not seem to have gained much

advantage from Iran, nor from Nigeria, who nationalised our oil without paying for it. If that is investment, it seems to be the worst we have ever made. The British universities are funded by the British rate and taxpayer, not from outer space.

(*Times Higher Education Supplement* 1979)

These were fighting words. Maurice and David Kogan, as leading educational and political commentators writing in 1983, could scarcely have foreseen the changes made to and within the UK system in the fifteen years that followed. Writing of the most pessimistic interpretation they stated,

The wider consequences of discouraging overseas students from attending British courses are likely to be serious. British universities lead the world in many academic disciplines, and many able scholars from overseas have received their undergraduate or graduate training in Britain. So, indeed, have many of the distinguished leaders of British Commonwealth countries. Science and technology students from overseas have learnt to respect British technology and have become accustomed to using British scientific and technical equipment. These ties will now be damaged, and our academic and technical markets diminished. The government's decision – one made by little Englanders – disregarded Britain's role in the world of ideas, education and science.

(Kogan 1983)

There can be no doubt of the problems that this decision caused both for the international students and for the universities. There can be no doubt either of the resource of imagination, compassion, liberality, energy and sheer commercial flair which was soon summoned to meet this difficult position.

A proactive approach

The status quo

There have been so many changes in the pattern of UK post-compulsory education provision since 1980 that it is worth remembering how the system was then configured. The binary line existed with universities on one side and the polytechnics and colleges of higher education on the other.[8] The percentage of the age cohort attending institutes of higher education stood at about 20 per cent. Large numbers of international students primarily from the Commonwealth nations studied at the universities paying the same tuition fee as the UK students. They were not 'recruited' but accepted. There was no limit set by the government on home undergraduate numbers. The polytechnics saw fewer of the overseas students than did the universities. London, Oxford and Cambridge accommodated a significant proportion of the overseas population. There was little corporate drive to increase overseas numbers – nor did there need to be, since well-qualified students came of their own volition. There was little institutional focus and very little specific organized expertise for these students.[9] Some colleagues were interested in them, the Christian communities and charitable trusts were exceptionally welcoming. Individual supervisors were helpful as in the main they had selected the students.[10] The colleges of Further Education (FE) were financed and administered by the local authorities and rarely saw international students. They were more likely to be working with and for ethnic minorities in the home community. Schools and colleges in the private sector occasionally accepted international pupils. By and large, the UK institutions offered proudly to the academic market place what they did well and generally without modification. London University, as a service to the Commonwealth, offered an early form of distance learning through its external degree system. That apart, the intellectually able – international royalty, together with international families of wealth and position and international recipients of aid – studied in the UK institutions in much the same way as did the UK students.

In 1981, as a result of the change to the fee, there were only 55,000 international students in the UK. The institutions did not agree with the legislation to raise the fees for all the obvious reasons rehearsed by Kogan above. They saw clearly that these international students would vanish unless effective action was taken. Action was taken, so that the pessimistic scenario envisaged by Dahrendorf did not come about. The universities eventually began to benefit from income generated by the new full-cost fees. The polytechnics designated as universities in the 1990s shared the financial bonus. The colleges of FE, released from local authority control, found themselves a market in vocational sub-degree and even degree work with international students.[11] Schools and colleges recognized opportunities for entry to this international business. Rich veins of well-qualified students who could afford the fees were tapped and scholarships directed at some equally gifted who could not. The commercial imperative led to a greater understanding of the needs of international students – both academic and cultural. The drive for customer-orientated, sensitive, clear marketing to attract international students brought spin-off benefits to the other student constituencies. The money available through fees enabled all parts of the institutions to develop for the good of the whole.

These are the positive outcomes. The dangers of acceptance of low standards, of short-term and crass approaches to the market, of unproductive competition, friction with indigenous student groups and deviation from educational objectives are all considered in later sections. The overall verdict is one of success through a combination of learning, caring and spending which is described in more detail in Chapter 5. In 1981, however, standing at the brink of what could have been disaster, the institutions addressed this problem by harnessing both external and internal resources.

The British Council

The British Council, established by the government in 1934, existed as the cultural and educational arm of diplomacy, bringing examples of British art and letters to many parts of the world and operating a series of well-regarded libraries.[12] It administered scholarships and aid to students and would have been known to a significant but small proportion of colleagues in the higher education institutions. The Council's role in the period from 1979 to the present day has been an evolving one.[13] British Council papers chart its progress from the December 1979 meeting when

> the Director General reported that the proposed increase in fees for overseas students to a total of up to £5,000 per annum (depending on discipline) would have a profound effect on the Council's awards. The universities were also seriously concerned about the probable loss of students from overseas. He had, therefore, arranged a meeting with members of the Committee of Vice-Chancellors and Principals on 8 February at which the whole problem would be discussed.
>
> (British Council 1979)

So it all began. By the time of the meeting of the British Council Board on 1 April 1980 the planned meeting with the CVCP had taken place and the Director General, Sir John Llewellyn, reported, '. . . that the rate of increase in overseas students had already slowed down and was expected to level off. It was agreed that the Council should distribute publicity material for the scheme prepared by the

CVCP through its offices overseas' (British Council 1980). The Council noted the effect that a decline in overseas student population would be likely to have on the balance of payments. It was noted, too, that the House of Commons Select Committee on Education was presently considering the matter as part of its study on higher education. At the same time, the Board established a Standing Committee for University and Higher Education Overseas, which would represent universities, polytechnics and 'other institutions primarily concerned with degree courses'. This marked the beginning of a special relationship between the British Council and the collective body of representatives from higher education, at least 15 of which representatives would attend the new Standing Committee (ibid.). Simultaneously, the British Council would establish 'a recognisable unit (which might be called Higher Education Division) to co-ordinate and execute programmes of work hitherto the responsibility of the British Council and the inter-university council' (ibid.). Early in 1981, the Council, at the Ditchley Park Conference, reviewed its own position, stating that 'the Council wanted to be sure that it discharged its functions effectively in the fast changing world of the 80s'. And for this, 'the views and judgements on future priorities of people with wider perspectives, were important' (British Council 1981). The following year saw a concern, soon dispelled, that overseas students would have to pay for healthcare. In the same year, the Overseas Student Trust Report was discussed. This established with authority

> the importance of overseas students to Britain's national interest. It acknowledged the long term friendship of overseas countries arising from the education in Britain of many of their political, administrative and business leaders; and a connection between training in Britain and future orders for British goods and services.
>
> (British Council 1982)[14]

The Trust had recommendations to make concerning government liberality in relation to the full-cost fees. The government's response to the Trust report was, fortunately, supportive and in February it was stated,

> the Government has, therefore, decided to increase its support for overseas students by £46 million over the next three years. This will involve an additional sum of £25 million from the contingency reserve and reallocation of resources within the aid programme, amounting to £21 million.[15]

The influential and expert view indicated in *A Policy for Overseas Students* is worth noting at this stage. It was discussed by the British Council at its meeting in August 1983 when the full statement was debated by the Council in confidence as an annex to the agenda papers. The formal position remained as follows:

> The Government's policy on overseas students since 1979 has been to replace the haphazard and indiscriminate subsidy given previously to overseas students in general by a more selective and discriminating policy. Full cost fees have gone hand in hand with continued substantial support to students and trainees from developing countries under the aid programme. With the concession of home fees to students from EC countries and to refugees and with British Council and other scholarship schemes, including the Overseas Research Students Awards schemes, the Government believes that this approach is the right one. They note that it is widely accepted that there can be no return to the previous policy of indiscriminate and open ended subsidy; that it is not desirable to control overseas student numbers by a system of quotas; and that a principal mechanism should be schemes of support targeted at particular groups of students.
>
> (British Council 1983a)

At a time of reduction in real terms for its own budget, the British Council continued to stress the need to address the plight which the universities and the country faced. In 1983 it stressed again,

> The policy relating to overseas student fees has emphasised the importance of marketing our educational services overseas. The Council has discussed this with the universities and polytechnics. It will be necessary to develop more vigorous and organised support to British institutions by making the range, variety and relevance of their courses known in a number of countries as still a 'best buy', even at the increased cost.
>
> (British Council 1983b)

At the meeting of the Board on 3 April 1984, the key decisions were taken to set up the pilot projects for the Education Counselling Service (ECS). The Board now saw the British Council as key to the promotion of British higher education. It was noted that while the Council already provided information on British further and higher education facilities more needed to be done. Additional effort was required.

However, since the introduction of full cost fees, Britain's position in the educational field has been challenged in many areas by competitors, notably the USA which has established counselling centres in many key countries and actively promotes American higher education in government departments, industry, universities and schools.

(British Council 1984)

It was, therefore, agreed that in 1984/85 two projects for the Education Counselling Service should be established in Singapore and Malaysia with a further three projects the following year in Hong Kong, Indonesia and Brazil. In fact, Hong Kong was immediately named as the third centre. It was agreed that the proposed service would be market-orientated and would be established to meet the needs of both British and overseas clients. British clients would include all the subscribing institutions and those further education colleges which were working in conjunction with the universities and polytechnics in offering first degree access programmes. At this point it was noted that the UK clients would be asked to contribute. It is interesting to note that at this point, too, the possibility of conflict with private agencies was raised. The Council was happy to say at this juncture that 'evidence suggests that the majority of institutions would prefer that the Council as a public body . . . should act on their behalf' (ibid.). During the discussion the views of the CVCP and the Committee for International Co-operation in Higher Education (CICHE) were conveyed. Issues were debated then that have reoccurred time and again in the history of the Council's relationship with the subscribers. It was believed that the initiative would stand a greater chance of success if all eligible institutions participated. The institutions, too, saw the proposal 'not so much as an extension of the Council's current work as a substantial change in kind' (ibid.). A move from a passive to an active role was urgently needed if Britain was to compete effectively with the enormous efforts made by other countries, particularly in the prime markets like Hong Kong. It is interesting to note, too, for those who were party to the debate on fee levels in 1996, that subscribers had suggested that 'a combination of subscription and capitation fee might emerge as a preferred alternative' (ibid.). It was very much hoped that the ECS project could be started in the autumn of 1984 to ensure suitable entrants to the institutions in autumn 1985. And so it all began.[16]

At the end of the first year of ECS operation, the British Council Board concluded that it was a 'modest success story for which all those concerned should be congratulated'. At this stage, personal support had been received from senior figures in both Hong Kong and Malaysia and 72 subscribers had participated in the scheme as opposed to a pre-launch estimate of 24. The service would continue into its second year in 1985/86 with 51 firm subscriptions already paid up and it was expected that numbers joining and rejoining would exceed the original 72.[17] It was agreed to wait until the close of the second year before a full evaluation would be held. It is interesting, as one looks back at this time of development, to note the words of Professor Sloman making his contribution to the discussion. There will certainly be feelings now of déjà vu!

> He also wished to add three cautionary notes. First, that the impression should not be given that the prime purpose of the scheme was financial. Second, that care should be taken when presenting figures. The total fee income resulting from the students recruited was impressive, but it was impossible to say how many of these students would have come whether or not there had been a Counselling Service. Third, that while there was probably total acceptance by the British subscribers of the Council's role in promotion, their role in placement was not so clear and problems might arise in the future. Professor Sloman advised that the Council should consolidate the service as at present provided before considering any enlargement of the constituency of subscribers beyond the universities and polytechnics.'
> (British Council 1985a)

Further debate on this topic spoke of the dangers of 'over zealous recruiting', of the widespread suspicion of second-rate overseas students being accepted in preference to good home students and problems of double standards and adverse publicity. Board members were pleased to see that the central effort of the British Council would stop any possible free-for-all by individual institutions. The objectives and methodology of the ECS placement services can be found in the endnotes.[18] In October 1985 the Council received, in confidence, the report of the first year of the Educational Counselling Service. The placement service purpose, method, staffing, selection and training, funding, and costs were discussed. It was noted with pleasure that the ECS had achieved the five principal objectives set for its first year. These were:

1.1 to operate a professional student counselling and promotion service in higher education in Malaysia, Singapore and Hong Kong in order to provide a practical means of increasing the numbers of students from these countries choosing Britain for their higher education

1.2 to establish the British Council as the key source of advice and information in these countries for potential students and their sponsors, and to secure the support of their governments and higher education authorities

1.3 to secure the support of the majority of British universities and polytechnics for the service and to secure sufficient financial support through subscriptions to cover the costs of the operation

1.4 to develop a programme of Council organised promotional visits, seminars and exhibitions overseas and to support and coordinate visits by individual British institutions

1.5 to use the experience gained from the ECS for education promotion work by the British Council elsewhere.

(British Council 1985b)

By 1985 the ECS was preparing publicity releases and promotion plans. Missions were being organized of a general and specific nature, together with promotional visits and major conventions. From this point the subscribers recognized the importance of the British Council and the list of activities and endeavours increased. The resourcing, the staffing, the level of interest and the spread of activity which the ECS service offers in partnership to subscribers in 1998 is almost unrecognizable from the tentative steps of 1984. Desmond Lauder, now Director Hong Kong, but in 1984–6 Assistant Representative, ECS Singapore, was instrumental in establishing one of these pilot offices. They had been concerned that the Singaporeans would not respond well to overt promotion and were surprised when the Singaporean students and sponsors seemed happy with this approach. As long as the issue was one of quality, he recalled, there was no difficulty. The new office held an exhibition as one of its earliest activities but this was a small-scale affair using a hotel ballroom and tables and chairs rather than booths or stands. There were few International Offices present then and many academic staff were taking on the role of coordination. In those early days, too, the Education Counsellors could spend 40 minutes with each potential student. The polytechnics were experiencing difficulty with recognition. His memory of the period is that by 1986 the Singaporeans and indeed the nations competing with the British were beginning to 'sit up and take notice' (Lauder 1998).

The process of development and expansion continued and in 1990 an Assistant Director General of the British Council noted with pleasure when reviewing the advances made by the institutions,

The British Council has been active in encouraging, aiding and abetting those changes. Its most notable contribution has been the move away from its traditional responsive information role to an active promotional one in important markets ... It offers individual counselling to potential students, organises massive high-profile education fairs, arranges inward and outward missions and supplies regular market intelligence!

(Vale 1990)

The competition

The government, by its 1979 legislation, left the universities with the possibility of the loss of £100 million a year in fee subsidy from overseas students. The institutions took an entrepreneurial stance and with the British Council and others like the United Kingdom Council for Overseas Student Affairs (UKCOSA)[19] fought back to market their quality product in a positive and proactive manner. One external spectator reviewing the whole position in 1989 commented,

even more important than government action have been the entrepreneurial efforts of the universities themselves. Encouraged by government decisions that increasingly allow them to 'market' their educational services to foreign students at competitive tuition rates, the universities and, increasingly, the polytechnics have become aggressive marketers on the international scene. While their continued energies in recruiting foreign students have actually increased the numbers of postgraduate students beyond their 1979 levels and have helped give stability to British graduate programmes, their educational goals have seemed subordinate to their financial needs. Their open commercialism is a manifestation of what we shall see elsewhere in this study: a shift from a 'classical' internationalism, stressing ideals of mutual understanding, towards a frankly cash benefit motive.

(Chandler 1989)

Her conclusion, too, was then that Britain in the early 1980s 'discussed foreign student policy almost exclusively in pragmatic terms ... lacking a broader philosophical base'. That was written only a few years after the external environment had changed so dramatically for the UK institutions. In 1987 surveys were taking place on the level of marketing expertise available for the international promotion exercise and were finding it wanting. 'Competing in the

world's market place for students exposes British higher education to very public scrutiny of its ability to meet the challenge
of both recruiting in and retaining a share of the market' (Eggins
1988: 126).

A more optimistic perspective on developments in the last twelve
years can be found in other sections of this book.

When the UK institutions decided to, or were compelled to, go
out into the international student market place, they did not do so
in isolation. Competitors in the shape of France, Germany, Japan,
Australia and North America were already active – not all seeking
full fee-paying students but all seeking to swell their home student
communities with appropriately qualified students from overseas.
Policy in these countries has shifted during the period, from open
welcome to a regulated quota system in some, from strict requirements for fees to generous scholarship provision in others.

The UK looked ever more closely at the skills and techniques
employed by Australian and North American colleagues and their
apparent unified approach and government-backed response. Gradually, the UK institutions offered a more cohesive and sensible face to
potential students and their sponsors, with clearer indications as to
progression, more professional attitudes to other institutions and
more unified action with government. The DTI funding for marketing and the 1998 British government matching scholarship schemes
for students from Malaysia, Thailand, Indonesia and Korea have
done much to consolidate this improved image. As will be considered in later sections, successful marketing of the education product
depends upon more than the conditions pertaining in the individual
institutions or the promotional skills of their officers. Economic,
political, social and even meteorological factors affect the popularity
of the country in the eyes of international students and their sponsors.
The strength of the currency; involvement in international disputes;
media coverage on ethnic minority or immigrant worker problems; a
crime wave in a student city; injudiciously phrased political dogma;
or even a series of bad summers can influence student choice of
destination. When France, Germany, Japan, Australia or the USA
receives a bad student press, Britain benefits and, of course, this
works in reverse. All of these countries have experienced a similar
history over the last seventeen years. It began with a restriction of
foreign student flow at the end of the 1970s and the beginning of
the 1980s, followed by much more welcoming policies in recent
years. As Alice Chandler explains,

The methodologies for constriction differed: full cost fees in Great
Britain, admission requirements in France, visa regulations in

Germany, quota and fees in Australia, and differential provin-
cial tuition in Canada, but the motivations were always much
the same. The flow of foreign students was perceived as getting
out of hand. The cost of their education, their perceived rivalry
for limited university spaces, their potential competitiveness in
a declining job market, their racial and ethnic differences from
the general population, their lumpy geographical distribution
within the host country, and their inevitable involvement in
broader issues of immigration, were all causes for concern.

(Chandler 1989)

Fortunately, for liberal humanitarian reasons in all cases, the
draconian statements at the beginning of this period were moder-
ated during the years immediately following 1980 and a more bal-
anced approach has now been taken by all of these countries. The
competition continues to be intense. During the 1980s and 1990s
there was worldwide recognition of the many benefits of a successful international recruitment strategy. The institutions in the UK
and the British Council recognized that

All Britain's competitor countries are active in this area, promoting their educational systems, recruiting fee paying overseas
students, and expanding their scholarship schemes. The Amer-
icans are certainly in the lead in this, and much can be learned
from their approach . . . They offer a 'from here to eternity' opportunity   Their material is user friendly and alluring . . . They
have no inhibitions when it comes to marketing and selling
their wares . . . And the skill and effort of individual colleges
and universities are complemented by a global network of official
or quasi-official information/counselling services. Their after sales
service is impressive . . . and the whole effort is underpinned by
massive scholarship programmes.

(Vale 1990)

Conclusion

The government legislation on full-cost overseas fees created a difficulty for the tertiary education sector in the UK. The institutions
themselves recognized the difficulty and during the 1980s, with the
British Council and other agencies, began to address it. During the
1990s, the strength of the international competition was evident

and during that decade the UK players acknowledged what was required of their own system in order to compete successfully in the global market.

The entrepreneurial institution, which has emerged in the UK in many sectors in the last fifteen years, has attempted to respond with imagination, skill and integrity to match the strengths perceived in our competitors, as the quotation above described them. In 1990 it was said, when reviewing the position:

> Our educational institutions and country could not afford to lose the benefits (of international recruitment). Thus there arose a specialist category for the new professionals, that of international education. At the same time the 'entrepreneurs' were joined by a stream of staff whose background was primarily in the caring and support services . . . there has been a rapprochement between these two approaches and all now agree that marketing and caring are two facets of the same diamond.
>
> (Warner 1990)

The chapters that follow concentrate on the development, refinement and cohesion of these activities.

Endnotes

1 The 'studium generale', also known as the 'studium universale' or 'studium commune', came to mean a school where there were organized facilities for study with the capability of attracting students from a wider community outside the immediate locality. Latin was the common language. By 1300 the term had come to mean: 'a guild organisation of master or students or of masters and students combined [which] . . . in addition to arts, offered instruction in at least one of the superior faculties of law, theology or medicine' (Cobban 1975).
2 Rashdall had written in the 1930s a three-volume comprehensive review of the medieval institutions entitled *The Universities of Europe in the Middle Ages*.
3 The Robbins Committee stated in their report of 1963 that 'Courses of higher education should be available for all those who are qualified by ability and attainment to pursue them and who wish to do so' (Robbins 1963: para. 31).
4 The civic university movement can be studied through such books as Armytage (1955) and Mansbridge (1922). Individual histories of civic universities like Reading, Nottingham and Sheffield have also been well recorded. The following table indicates dates of opening and establishment.

Table 1.1 Dates of opening and chartering of universities and university colleges in England for the period up to 1958

Institution	Date of opening	Date of establishment as independent university
Oxford	–	12th century
Cambridge	–	13th century
London		1836
University College	1828	–
King's College	1831	–
Durham	1833	1833
King's College, Newcastle	1871	–
Manchester	1851	1903[1]
Birmingham	1880	1900
Liverpool	1882	1903[1]
Leeds	1874	1904[1]
Sheffield	1880	1905
Bristol	1876	1909
Reading	1892	1926
Nottingham	1881	1948
Southampton	1902[2]	1951
Hull	1928	1954
Exeter	1901[3]	1955
Leicester	1921	1957
North Staffordshire	1950	–

Notes: 1 The colleges at Manchester, Liverpool and Leeds formed part of the
Victoria University wihch was established in 1880.
2 The Hartley Institute at Southampton was established in 1850.
Source: Simmons (1959).

5 Sir John Lubbock MP was Chairman of the 1889 *ad hoc* Committee on Grants to University Colleges. The quotation is from his article in the *Times*. This view was repeated by Dearing some 110 years later. The same interdependence between the level of education and national economic health was described:

> ... nations will need, through investment in people, to equip them-selves to compete at the leading edge of economic activity. In the future, competitive advantage for advanced economies will be in the quality, effectiveness and relevance of their provision for education and training, and the extent of their shared commitment to learning for life.
>
> (NCIHE 1997: para. 24)

6 Economists of education have written at some length on this subject. Bowen, Kendrick and Denison all reflected on the benefit to the individual, as did Robbins:

But if finance is provided by outright subsidy from public funds, it is said a new position of principle is created: the recipient of the subsidy is being put in a position to command a higher income in virtue of taxes paid, in part at least, by those whose incomes are smaller . . .'
(Robbins 1963: paras 642, 647)

Dearing also refers to this: 'Higher education has proved to be an excellent personal investment with a return averaging between 11 and 14 per cent and we expect it to continue to be a good investment, even after further expansion' (NCIHE 1997: para. 25).

7 The following table indicates this percentage figure from 1920/21 to 1948/49.

Table 1.2 Parliamentary Grant to the English university institutions in actual figures and as a percentage of total university income from 1920 to 1949

Year	Parliamentary Grant	
	Actual figure (£)	*Percentage of total university income*
1920/1	686,524	31.8
1921/2	896,192	34.6
1923/4	906,051	34.7
1924/5	930,657	35.0
1925/6	1,400,613	37.2
1926/7	1,380,955	35.7
1927/8	1,394,785	35.4
1928/9	1,401,178	34.5
1929/30	1,424,820	34.0
1930/1	1,574,116	34.1
1931/2	1,563,558	33.7
1932/3	1,551,885	33.1
1933/4	1,545,241	32.7
1934/5	1,552,356	32.0
1935/6	1,564,938	32.4
1936/7	1,739,288	34.0
1937/8	1,785,659	34.2
1938/9	1,809,725	33.9
1939/40	1,854,057	36.3
1945/6	3,966,381	48.2
1946/7	5,496,414	52.4
1947/8	7,530,785	57.7
1948/9	8,618,261	59.1

Notes: Parliamentary Grant includes Treasury (UGC) Grant and grant from the Ministry of Education and other government departments.
Source: Adapted from UGC Returns for the years indicated, income table.

8 The distinction which ended at the beginning of the 1990s was one which occasioned considerable and interesting debate on the nature of higher education and the quest for standards and criteria in higher education.

> Although consideration of standards has to be focused on university processes and understandings, the major change heralded by the post war developments was the direct and continuing concern of the newly designated public sector institutions of higher education, and the processes of validation and review which they promoted . . . The polytechnics designated at the end of the 1960s needed to attain, redefine and demonstrate standards in very different institutional contexts.
>
> (Moodie 1986)

9 Margaret Kinnell, in her marketing study included in *Restructuring Higher Education* (Eggins 1988: 125), states, 'Co-ordinated marketing activities within British higher education are still relatively novel, although they are becoming of greater significance.'

10 Schemes, such as HOST, came into existence in 1987, founded by the British Council, the FCO and the Victoria League. 'Many (students) have commented that the scheme has transformed their view of us and their whole attitude to their stay in this country' *Journal of International Education* (January 1991, supplementary issue).

11 'Since incorporation in 1993 there has been a significant increase in the number of Further Education Colleges promoting themselves in the international market place. This is a reflection of both the opportunities offered by an expanding international market and the constraints placed upon potential growth by the funding restrictions within the UK' (Broxtowe College, Nottingham, *Annual Report 1997*: 5).

12 *The British Council 1996/97* (leaflet) stated:

> The British Council was established by the Government in 1934 . . . The British Council, registered in England as a charity, is the United Kingdom's international network for education, culture and development services . . . The Council's work is designed to establish long-term and world-wide partnerships and to improve international understanding . . . it is an integral part of the UK's overall diplomatic and aid effort.

13 The papers and minutes of the British Council Committees and Board in the Council's archives were made available for this book. Sources of quotations are listed in the Bibliography.

14 Comment on the excellent work of the Trust at this period can be found in the Alice Chandler book, *Obligation or Opportunity: Foreign Student Policy in Six Major Receiving Countries* (1989): 'That Britain found a clear path out of what seemed insoluble difficulties in 1983 was due in large measure to the patient and skilled diplomacy of the Overseas Students Trust (OST).'

The OST was a small voluntary organization dedicated to promoting the education of overseas students in Britain. Its proposals outlined in the report recognized that subsidy in tuition fees for international students was no longer possible but recommended a structured and targeted scholarship programme of which the Pym Package was the key point. This was focused particularly on Hong Kong, Malaysia and Cyprus.

15 Statement to the House of Commons by Secretary of State for Foreign and Commonwealth Affairs (8 February 1983).

16 In the digest of responses to the package, several universities responded with enthusiasm to the production of the first British Council Market Surveys: 'Factual information of this nature gathered in the field by your Representatives will help us to determine our own marketing strategy and will save us a considerable amount of difficult market research' Sir Edward Parks, Vice-Chancellor, Leeds University, 1 November 1983).

Others commented favourably on the 'important links with universities' that the British Council was thereby creating (G.E. Chandler, Registrar, University of Nottingham).

17 Board Minutes (April 1985):

2 Subscriptions per Institution

(1) A total of 90 potential subscribers ie 60 members of CVCP and 30 members of CDP in England and Wales has been assumed in calculating subscriptions per institution. This estimate does not include non-CVCP represented colleges nor Scottish Central Institutions.

(2) At a subscription of £5,000 per institution the breakeven points would be:
1984/5 to cover total costs of £117,055
– 24 subscribers
1985/6 to cover total costs of £391,480
– 78 subscribers
This last figure represents a take-up rate of 87%

(3) In practice, over 24 subscriptions are expected in 1984/85 and rather fewer than 78 in 1985/86. On this basis the subscription of £5,000 can be maintained in 1985/86, carrying forward any 1984/85 subscriptions (beyond the breakeven point) to the following year. Additional subscriptions beyond this point would lower costs for subscribers.

18 Board Minutes (1 October 1985):

PLACEMENT SERVICES

Purpose – to secure undergraduate and postgraduate places in British universities and polytechnics for suitably qualified overseas applicants

Method – applicants filtered at the counselling stage will be interviewed by the student counsellor to determine suitability for placement action. The identification of the British institution will depend on the expressed preference (if any) of the student, course suitability, geographical preference and availability of places

- final recommendation on placement will be taken by the placement coordinator in London who will maintain up-to-date information on availability of places by course and institution
- for postgraduate placements a standard proforma will be used. For first degree placements the service will operate through facilities to be provided by UCCA
- English language testing will be provided to subscribers (at cost) as an additional service if required

Staffing – the balance of 50% of the time of the staff working on promotion will be allocated to placement in each overseas country
- 100% of the time of a Grade F placement coordinator in Higher Education Division liaising with universities and polytechnics
- 100% of the time of a Grade G equivalence officer in head-quarters

Selection and training
Staff working on placement will also cover promotion and will be selected and trained for both tasks.

Funding
All costs overseas and at headquarters would be covered by subscribing institutions.

19 The role of UKCOSA will be discussed in more detail in Chapter 4. An understanding of the breadth of this association's work, publication and scholarship can be gathered from the scope of its writings. In 1992/93, for example, its publications included *Good Practice: The Role of Student Unions; Have Dependants – Must Travel: A Guide to the Special Needs of Overseas Students with Dependants; Can We Help with the Washing Up?; Internationalising the British; Orientation within the Institution: A DIY Guide to Welcoming International Students; Beyond the Institution: International Students in the Community; Meeting Religious Needs; Homeward Bound.*

UKCOSA is a registered charity established in 1968 to promote educational mobility and to provide support to international students and the professionals who work with them. It is an independent, non-profit making membership organization which provides information, advice and training about the recruitment, education and support of international students.

2

MARKETING THE PRODUCT: CREATING A STRATEGIC PLAN FOR THE INSTITUTION

Introduction

Bearing in mind all the issues raised in Chapter 1, the institution has decided that it would benefit from having a proportion of its student community drawn from overseas. Such a diversity would accord, and not be at variance with, its agreed long-term objectives. Institutions of further and higher education are now well accustomed to developing, articulating and promulgating a plan that incorporates academic, physical and financial factors, generally on a rolling basis. Raising the right questions in the debates which must necessarily precede such a plan is a key element of successful recruitment.

The background to the planning debate and the need for a strategic approach is now known and accepted in education's management methodology. In the UK, a report prepared by tertiary sector administrators in 1989 agreed that

> strategic planning is concerned with the long-term relationships between the organisation's goals and the environment or 'market' in which it operates. In order to define its relationship with the environment, an institution would be expected to establish its mission (a statement of its overall purpose in the context of its environment) . . . an institution which wishes to be and to remain effective, needs to be aware of changes in the world outside which may affect it, and to think about the relationship of these external changes to its internal . . . activities.
>
> (CUA/APA 1989: 3)[1]

As discussed in the opening chapter, UK institutions – while not instigating the full-fee initiative – have quickly adapted to benefit financially from the change. It can be supposed at this stage that in the UK whichever of the political parties is in government will retain the full fee-paying concept. As this has coincided with a period of straitened resourcing for the institutions, it has inevitably been regarded with different degrees of enthusiasm and candour as 'the golden goose'. All institutions will recognize the educational and academic advantages of a multinational community of scholars, as well as the global imperative to make available useful technology and so help alleviate poverty and ignorance. This has always been widely accepted. It is the income-generating aspect identified and emphasized after 1980 which requires careful consideration in the plan.

After years of growth of the market, it is all too easy to regard international fee income as a tap that can be opened more widely whenever a shortfall in any other area of income is expected during the budgetary round. If home undergraduate numbers are capped in the allocation of MASN (Maximum Aggregate Student Number),[2] if part-time recruitment falls away, if a decline in consultancy income is anticipated, or if additional income streams are required to capitalize or maintain projects, then unrealistic expectations can suddenly be placed on international recruitment. In principle, it may be a very good thing to expand international student numbers, but a headlong, cash-driven demand for this increase is liable to ignore key considerations. Without giving thought to these considerations, debating them within the institution and embedding them into a thoughtfully resourced strategic plan, the institution may experience short-term gain but little hope of long-term achievement.

The institution must have clear sight of its objectives, its rationale and its ethos. To some degree, the advent of significant numbers of international students will inevitably change identity, priorities and image. An institution that seeks success in international recruitment must believe, at all levels, that the changes will be predominantly for the better and to the advantage of *all* concerned. Such changes will not be achieved without thought, resourcing, effort and, most importantly, proper prior planning. Any such planning should indicate not only target numbers, but also nationality mix, quotas, course provision and course delivery.

Components of the plan

Any institution begins its international recruitment process with a portfolio of existing courses, a cadre of established staff and a resource of buildings and equipment. It will decide, either before it embarks on recruitment and/or as it continues to grow, how much of its international student target should be met by 'in-fill' and how much by new course provision. Any decision it makes is likely to affect the shape and the character of the institution.

Recruitment within existing parameters

At the margins

Most UK sixth-form colleges, and all the institutions of further and higher education, were established for the use and benefit of those living in the UK. This is obviously not true of language schools, whose courses are in general tailor-made for international students. For reasons explained earlier, the existing provision has capacity for students in larger numbers than presently can be recruited from the UK base and, again for the reasons listed, it is to everyone's advantage to fill this capacity with appropriately qualified international students. The decision to recruit to existing courses is, therefore, a fairly straightforward one, especially when the programmes already attract robust numbers of home students. In these cases, an increase in overall numbers can be seen as marginal in terms of staff–student ratio, classroom and laboratory capacity. Classes for top secondary school students in economics, undergraduate courses in electrical engineering and masters courses in computer science, could all fall within this category. In addition, many courses in this category can be viewed as culturally neutral: electrical engineering graduates returning to Birmingham, Athens, Ankara or Kuala Lumpur will all need to be equally familiar with the same undiscriminating law of electrolysis!

Quotas and proportions

It is only when the number of international students grows beyond the scope of existing facilities that issues of degradation of staff–student ratios (SSR) or appointment of extra staff, of overcrowding or new build or parallel teaching have to be faced. At every stage there is a tension between cost and benefit. Within the institution, too, there will be discussion of 'proportions' and the percentage of international students that can be properly accepted within the community. Are these quotas to be set departmentally or across the institution as a whole? There is obviously a difference between 20 out of 30 undergraduate law students coming from Malaysia, and

200 out of 300 social science students coming from Asia as a whole. There is a difference, too, according to the quality of the students recruited. No one doubts that international students inevitably create a disproportionate amount of work for the institution. Those who teach them are often required to spend more time with individual international students outside the classroom in explanation, clarification and general reassurance. Other institutional facilities, such as the library, can be similarly stretched. Unless the institution, for what we hope is a multiplicity of good reasons, has an absolute commitment to the enterprise, having considered all these 'costs', then difficulties, failures and antagonisms will occur. This is not an undertaking to be entered into lightly.

There can be no one quota which is good for all courses in all institutions. The London School of Economics has a long tradition of excellence with a high percentage of international postgraduates on some of its most prestigious courses. Indeed, many of the home students on these programmes would regard the presence of these international students as being one of the benefits of study at LSE. Other institutions with other courses and other catchment areas may find such a percentage unsupportable. When deciding on the mix, too, the institution needs to be aware of the international student perception. An undergraduate coming from Singapore may well have elected to study overseas in order to gain experience of life in another country. It can be counterproductive and disappointing if the whole period is spent with friends made only in the Singaporean Student Society, in self-catering accommodation with a high percentage of Singaporeans and in classrooms surrounded by compatriots. If the mix is right, however, the stimulation of being part of a postgraduate group whose relevant work experience covers Europe, America and Asia can be unrivalled, resulting in exciting interchange and a true broadening of perspective.

Appropriate quality

The quality of the student recruited – both academic and linguistic – will also affect the desired quota. Is it the institution's wish to recruit international students with the same level of proven intellectual ability as the home contingent, or simply of sufficient ability satisfactorily to complete the programme? There can be no moral justification for recruiting students who are judged to be incapable of completing the programme. Apart from the humanitarian issues, there can only be the briefest of short-term financial gains in such irresponsibility. It has been proved on so many occasions that bad news about unhappy and unsuccessful students travels so much more widely and quickly than the more numerous examples of satisfaction. If the institution, therefore, agrees only to accept competent students it must look at its own level of operation and decide at what level to pitch international recruitment. What are the entry scores of the home cohort? How much support is already offered for remediation? How quickly are formal assessments introduced in the programme? This issue has raised questions as to the pressures which the modular system in HE places on international students in the early months of study. All these issues need to be considered before decisions on entry level can be made. Other professional or quasi-academic issues may well have to be addressed in determining these levels. These will include, in medical and health science courses for example, the sensibility of patients, the pressures on other professionals where placements are required and safety in laboratories and workshops.

Language competence

Academic qualifications cannot be considered separately from linguistic ability. As long as the institutions are conducting their classes in English and requiring work to be submitted and assessed in that language, an adequate level of English language must be required at the point of entry to the programme. This does not mean on entry to the institution, as pre-course language training is often available. It does not mean either that the same level of language is required for every level of study or for every discipline. The case can be made that the linguistic demands of a one-year taught masters course are different from – and may be higher than – those required on registration for a three-year research degree. Language competence as a factor in pastoral concern and a care for student welfare are discussed in a later chapter, as are language improvement options. In writing its plan, the institution should ask these questions and must shape its policy as a result of the answers it receives.

Recruitment to new programmes

Up to this point, in relation to international students, the institution may only have looked at the possibility of in-filling. Places are available in Advanced Level (A Level)[3] classes or on undergraduate and postgraduate programmes, and there is a possibility of recruiting international students to fill them. The next stage is reached when the institution considers whether to offer what it has to the market, or to investigate what the market requires. It may then decide to meet market need by creating new programmes from the portfolio of academic talent and experience at its disposal. These are matters which, debated at one level, touch upon the fundamental purpose of the institution, its perceived strengths, its core business and its responsibilities to the local and national community.

Foundation courses – rationale and content

The emergence of the foundation/access/bridging course is one example of an area where expressed international need was recognized and addressed. In many countries, the school leaving qualifications (often taken after 12 rather than 13 years of full-time schooling) assess a breadth, rather than a depth of knowledge. Students will study 10 or 11 subjects rather than three or at maximum four, as in the UK Advanced Level examinations. The increasingly popular International Baccalaureate (IB) courses fall between these two systems.[1] The higher education systems in these countries match the secondary school systems by compensating with an additional undergraduate year. The best-recognized example of this system is that of the USA. Others include those found in the Middle East, Japan, Thailand and India.

The Pakistani educational system follows this pattern, a comparative table for which follows. It is interesting to note that the British Council market report for this country, dated December 1997, includes the idea of the 'access year' and, after consultation with NARIC, equates international examinations from Pakistan to Ordinary Level (O Level) standard. It also notes that Foundation Courses are in demand (British Council 1997a).

Formerly, if UK institutions wished merely to offer what was available, they recruited to A Level classes and the students effectively 'lost' a year. In many cases the students considered this worthwhile since they had an added opportunity for acculturation by residence and studying in English alongside groups of home students similarly preparing for entrance to UK higher education. Some colleges, conscious of understandable pressure from international sponsors and students, subsequently organized accelerated A Level groups or A Level classes which began at different times of the year. If the Indian school leavers completed their secondary education and had their examination results by Christmas, why not have an A Level intake which began classes in the UK in January? This led to a consideration of the value of the A Level to these groups of students. In Science and Engineering subjects there was a need for additional subject-based input, but was this still the case, for example, in the social sciences? UK students intending to study law, management or

Table 2.1 Comparison of Pakistan and UK education systems

Pakistan	Years of study	UK
	24	
	23	
	22	
	21	
	20	PhD
	19	3 or more years
PhD	18	
3 or more years	17	Postgraduate/Masters
Masters (2 years) MA, MSc, MCom	16	
Engineering College BE (4 years) — BA/BSc Hons	15	Undergraduate degrees BA (Hons) BSc (Hons)
Pass Degree (2 years) BA, BSc, BCom	14	
	13	A level/BTEC National GNVQ Advanced (age 16–18)
Higher secondary/Intermediate (age 15–17)	12	
	11	
	10	Senior school (age 11–16) GCSE
Secondary School SSC/Matric (age 10–14/15)	9	
	8	
	7	
	6	Junior school (age 7–11)
	5	
Primary school (age 5–9)	4	
	3	
	2	Infant school (age 5–7)
	1	

Source: Adapted from British Council (1997b)

economics did not require an A Level in any of these areas, but rather proven intellectual maturity and an ability to express themselves in written argument. There was no doubt that the higher education sector wanted able students from countries with the 12-year secondary system, and foundation/bridging/access programmes were created to meet the needs of the disciplines. For engineering, such courses concentrated on physics and mathematics. For architecture, they might include additional skills in creative art, and for social sciences, additional English language and breadth of reading. Some subjects, partly as a result of supply and demand, continued to require proof of ability through A Level or the IB. Medicine often finds itself in this group.

Foundation courses – location and programme

Further education institutions face the dilemma of whether to provide foundation courses as well as A Level programmes. Colleges catering only or primarily for international students also weighed up the opportunities. Understandably, institutions of higher education recognize the possibility of attracting international students either by working with the colleges or by running their own foundation programmes. Some of the friction between FE and HE arose over this disputed territory. Should higher education institutions offer sub-degree-level work? Do they have the skills for this level of teaching? The HE institutions must decide in looking at these opportunities what might be considered as dilution of mission, what is sensible in terms of SSRs and what is in the best interest of the students. As can be expected, and as is almost always the case, there is no simple answer. One college, whose role is the teaching of international students of the 16- to 19-year-old age group, has undertaken a study which indicates that foundation course students are at least as academically able as students who opt for the A Level route. Some university departments are not convinced by any foundation course concept, since it does not require students to sit national examinations with nationally agreed curriculum and assessment systems. They claim that, however rigorous the external examiner system employed for the foundation course, it inevitably lacks the objectivity of assessment in the A Level examinations. Debate on the quality of the A Level system may encourage more acceptance of the foundation course principle. From the student's point of view, application to a foundation course, especially with committed output, is straight forward and clearly analogous to the application procedures to universities in the USA, Australia and other 'competitor' countries. They believe they are being admitted to a seamless progression from sub-degree to degree study without encountering too many of the esoteric admission procedures.[5] Higher education institutions should consider how these younger students are to be taught most appropriately in a university environment, where they are to live and how their non-academic needs are best met.

Taught masters programmes

These are some of the issues raised when institutions decide on a mix of existing courses and new courses developed to meet the market. This is highlighted in higher education when considering the masters course portfolio. There is no doubt that the last ten years has seen a rapid increase in the numbers of international students recruited to one-year, full-time masters programmes overseas. Such masters programmes have obvious attractions for the international students and their sponsors. Their one-year duration in the UK makes them an affordable postgraduate qualification, achieved more rapidly and effectively in the UK than in the competitor countries. Their entry requirements are clear and application forms are straightforward. Their teaching styles and the modes of contact are familiar, with lectures and laboratories, seminars, tutorials and projects. They are 'safe' in that the programme expectations are understood, the research component of the dissertation is only a part of the whole and there is peer group companionship on the programme. They are not subject to the vagaries, however stimulating, of the individual supervisor, nor to the perceived isolation of, in particular, the arts-based PhD regime. They can offer a test of research potential, a conversion route from one subject to another,[6] a qualification from a prestigious UK institution completed in 12 months and a route to academic and professional advancement. Many even offer the added reassurance of the diploma safety net.

Any strategic institutional plan must decide:

- How many international students does it wish to include on its existing or as yet to be developed taught masters courses?
- Will it increase the number of these courses and so, perhaps, debase the currency? Guidance on the numbers of credits which can be awarded for the masters degree from final year undergraduate modules has helped to emphasize the quality issue.
- Will the institution develop generic modules on such programmes, which will allow a number of departments to share development time?
- Will it work to core subjects with electives that allow students to follow selected pathways in conjunction with core study?

- Will it set out to attract international students only, or to create a mix of home and overseas students?
- In the latter case, will it look for Funding Council acknowledgement and support? If it does, certain other criteria have to be met.[7]
- If the institution is to devote itself to courses directed solely at international students, will the students gain maximum benefit?
- Will the staff be competent to teach them?
- Will other staff be engaged?
- Will the library resources be adequate?
- Will the market prove volatile and the course become dependent on one sending source?

One of the most significant factors in the debate will be the institution's view of itself in the postgraduate field. In the UK, the Research Assessment Exercise (RAE), which ranks the quality of research undertaken subject by subject across all the institutions, has, among other outcomes, led to a clearer differentiation of research concentration and quality among institutions.[8] The regularity of the assessment and its importance to the finances and the future of the institutions means that it exerts a constant pressure on academic departments. Some departments will make strong and convincing cases that the highest marks on the RAE, and the maximum income from research and consultancy, can only be gained if academic colleagues are freed from the labour-intensive demands of masters teaching. Some academics, too, deny the need for progression in their disciplines via the masters programme and take the brightest students directly from bachelors degrees to the research programmes. On the other hand, some departments claim that the dissertation element of the masters course is a useful indicator of research potential. The institutional plan must assess the validity of these diverse views and address the need to meet them.

Every institution has a wide diversity of objectives. The institutional plan should indicate whether taught masters programmes are to be a central plank of the international recruitment platform or whether only a limited number of departments will offer them. This decision will touch not only on academic autonomy but also on the nature of corporate planning and this is mentioned again at the close of this chapter. At the same time, it must be remembered that, however desperate the individual institution's need for international students, it also has a clear national responsibility. The obligation to home students and to the region must be accorded its proper place within the plan. Some of the issues to be resolved include: the growth of the MBA and all its associated popular programmes; the tensions between a proliferation of taught courses at postgraduate level and the demands of research; the advantages of developing niche-taught courses directly responding to international requirements and thus attracting only international students.

Research degrees

The institution will be aware, of course, of some developments brought about after academic discussion, which have a significant bearing on international recruitment. One of these has been the changing shape of the PhD (Doctor of Philosophy) and the debate over the MRes (Master of Research). The British PhD was criticized by some overseas sponsors for a number of reasons that included a lack of structure, lack of direction, lack of consistency and, arising from these, a feeling of isolation and vulnerability on the student's part. Changes have been made to the shape of the British PhD – the taught element has been introduced, quality guidelines have been incorporated in connection with supervision and the research process. The essential requirement of the PhD remains unchanged. It is still necessary to demonstrate independence of thought. One research university's *Guide to Research Students and Supervisors* states:

> The degree of Doctor of Philosophy is awarded to candidates who have critically investigated and evaluated topics resulting in an independent and original contribution to knowledge, set out in a thesis which has been examined and defended in a viva voce examination. Candidates must show general knowledge of the wider field of scholarship to which their special topic belongs and knowledge of the appropriate research methodology. The originality of students' work may be in discovering new facts or examining existing facts or ideas critically, or in devising and conducting investigations into ideas supplied by others. The thesis must be a work of substance and worthy of publication, either as submitted or in a modified form.
>
> (University of Nottingham 1997: 10)

If students are not considered able to produce such a piece of research, they are not registered. Sponsors continue to be advised that it is the route for the most able students, but the procedures and systems are now more transparent and supportive. The MRes, once it becomes better known and more widely accepted, should offer a shorter and more focused route for research training, which will cater for those needing the research tools and skills without the requirement to demonstrate sustained and innovative research achievement.

Postgraduate foundation programmes may be marketed solely for international candidates and may offer components in English language, study skills, research training and academic enhancement. They would allow international students whose academic or linguistic ability was marginal or in doubt to embark upon a course of evaluation and remediation, success in which would lead to postgraduate registration.

The choices open to the planners are not easy ones. Consideration must be given to the longer term. The temptation to increase international recruitment to foundation courses in management in FE colleges is seductive. However, if this can cross-subsidise the 'access to work' class for the local disabled community, or be taught with the UK A Level group – thus enriching both home and overseas student experience – then it can accord with the institution's *raison d'être*. Almost all HE institutions could successfully increase recruitment to MBAs (Master of Business Administration) and MAs (Master of Arts) in Human Resource Management and Marketing. Very few will attract to a Masters programme in viking studies or musicology or to research in mathematics. It would be easy to accept a higher and higher proportion of international students in economics, law and management. Few from this category will register for chemistry or French. It would be simple to market courses directly geared to a specific sponsor's needs, but much more difficult and demanding to attract to a 'pure' rather than an 'applied' science area. The institution which adopts a strategy directed solely at an increase in overseas fee income risks losing its identity and, therefore, eventually the very asset which drew the international students to it in the first place. The debate on the role of higher education in society is not a new one. The platonic ideal has been tampered with, and perhaps even refined, through generations of informed discussion. The noted educationalist, Cardinal Newman, talked of raising the intellectual tone of society (1905); Flexner, the social commentator, claimed that practical importance was not a sufficient title to academic recognition (1930). Childs came closest to the late twentieth-century dilemma by saying, in speaking of the universities, 'Unless they are useful, they lose the world; and unless they are more than useful, they lose their souls' (Childs 1936). The institution that deliberately turns away from the market and pays no heed to international demand risks being unable to finance the level of activity which its corporate plan has determined. Somewhere between the two is the academically autonomous, market-aware, responsive yet proactive institution, which is neither vulnerable to the vagaries of international demand nor blind to the benefits it offers. Such an ideal institution must be apocryphal, but with a well-developed strategic plan many institutions will at least be able to justify the choices they make.

Timing and resourcing – how long and how much? ■

Having considered all these facts, the institution will have decided how many international students it wishes to recruit as well as in what proportion, at what level and on what courses. It will be satisfied that this recruitment is a proper objective and appropriate to the institution's overall aims.

It must now consider the timescale over which it wishes to see its recruitment goals achieved, the amount of resource it will put into meeting them, the methods by which it will convince its constituent parts of the rightness of the plan and encourage them to implement it, and the structure it will set up to achieve this. When active international recruitment was first formalized in the UK in the early 1980s, results could be achieved almost immediately. The Education Counselling Service (ECS) of the British Council was established with overseas offices in Hong Kong, Malaysia and Singapore. Visiting teams of academics began travelling, exhibitions were mounted and students began to flow again to the UK universities in spite of the full-cost fees. The polytechnics had a slightly more difficult task, since overseas students and sponsors reacted favourably to the title 'university' and gave less credibility in many subject areas to non-university institutions. Colleges of further education and other institutions were slower to embark on the process and, indeed, until the FE colleges became free of local education authority funding and management, there was little to be gained by overt and positive recruitment measures.

Institutions which began to be active in the 1980s reaped rewards to varying extents throughout that decade and into the 1990s. Those which began later found it a longer term process with more having to be invested to reap similar returns over a longer timescale. All those now involved in international recruitment have to include in their planning a selection of immediate, medium-term and long-term markets. Any strategy needs to include cash flow projections, area by area, and development by development. Some markets have always demanded a commitment to invest heavily and consistently. The British Council advises such commitment in, for example, Japan and Brazil. There are not only geographical markets but also sectoral interests. Undergraduate study of Medicine may be popular in one country, while FE skills packages may be sought after in another. Any institution seeking to gain a few immediate recruitment returns is more likely to visit selected schools or attend a popular exhibition than to set up a series of meetings with government sponsors, such as CONACYT or YÖK, in order to negotiate co-sponsored PhD degree programmes and collaborative research.[9] The strategy should include some longer term financial commitment both to marketing and to provision of essential facilities. It is almost pointless to make a single approach to a market – very little can be discovered and few contacts established without at least two visits. The converse of this, of course, is the need to show courage in pulling back from a market where little or nothing has been achieved after a number of visits. There is always the compulsive gambler's conviction that on the next trip all the losses will be recouped! Some markets are just not ready for some institutions and some institutions are just inherently unsuitable for some markets. A more detailed review of market analysis will be found in Chapter 3.

As with any other endeavour, the commitment and the resourcing assured by the institution will be key contributors to its long-term success. There must be clear understanding that only a proportion of endeavours in the international market will succeed. Some of the more successful of them can help to subsidize increased market penetration of the more difficult or competitive areas. A stop–go budget is not helpful. The strategic plan might touch upon the manner, or the formula, by which the international effort is to be resourced. Some institutions have decided to allocate to marketing a proportion of tuition fee income earned. Many accept a historical budget, inflation related. Others expect each project and initiative to be separately costed. It is a brave institution that continues with level funding when numbers decline, but in the private or commercial sector commentators speak favourably about companies 'tunnelling through' at times of recession with sustained or even increased resourcing. The public sector institutions should be aware of this model.

Responsibility and accountability for the plan

At this stage the institution will have a set of desired outcomes. It will also have a budget and timescale within which to achieve them. The next chapters will discuss some of the tactics that may be employed for the strategies to succeed. Questions now remain as to the lines of responsibility and accountability for meeting the target.

The management structure

Depending on the size of the institution, the degree of expenditure and the value of the expected return, there is a case to be made for establishing an international office or a named individual with the day-to-day responsibility for implementing the strategic plan. In some of the FE colleges this may come under marketing or external relations. In some other colleges, whose sole rationale is overseas recruitment, the Principal himself or herself may manage the exercise. In the institutions of higher education the type of management for this initiative will be established in the same way as that of a Development Office or new academic department. Some organizations have made it the responsibility of a Pro-Vice-Chancellor, either rotating or permanent. Some have placed such an office in the Registrar's department, some have appointed Deans of Admission to direct the activities, others Heads of Student Services, others academics who remain on academic appointments without academic responsibility, yet others professional administrators. Most work to and through a committee which fits into the overall institutional reporting structure and on which the head of the office, whoever that may be, sits in an executive capacity. The chair of the committee is normally not the head of the office. Each institution will create the structure that most efficiently and effectively represents its own ethos and accepted *modus operandi*. It is very important that the structure is clearly understood and publicized so that all members of the institution are familiar, not only with the plan but also with the established mechanisms which help deliver it. After that, as with most organizations, the informal contacts, liaisons and support that grow up around the office will contribute to its success.

Ownership

The issue of corporate responsibility for the plan touches upon the traditions in higher education institutions and the nature and character of the institution concerned. When a multi-million pound turnover company in the private sector delivers a five-year plan it is expected that departments, units and sectors are all signed up to that plan and regard corporate goals as the sole or at least paramount objective of each of the sections. For well-documented and laudable reasons, post-compulsory education in most countries is not run like that. In the UK, with the advent of decentralized budgets, and the importance of key academics to the delivery of the required

RAE results, it is even less likely to conform to this pattern. The good of the whole or the common weal is an interesting subject of debate in forums where democracy is valued, academic autonomy is revered, tenure is relied upon and some of the most articulate and highly intelligent individuals in the system can argue their points of view. While, for example, Special scientists may feel a strong loyalty to the discipline of Special science, they may feel less loyal to the University of X. The problem is exacerbated by the irregular pattern of international recruitment. It is likely that some disciplines will be asked to carry a greater load, since the nature of their subject is especially attractive to international students. It is, for example, probable that programmes in law will be popular with international students, while those in hispanic studies may be less so. If the numbers are to be delivered, departments have to realize that they are working within institutional parameters, and sometimes it may appear that the immediate good for their subject is overridden by the institutional good.

Sanctions

Any wise strategy will attempt to spread the recruitment load as evenly and as equitably as possible across the units within the institution. With enthusiasm and purpose, many departments perceived as unpopular have found real markets. Goodwill can only produce partial success and, in addition, for the sake of the institution as a whole, there may need to be a series of sanctions – carrot or stick – to encourage all sections to make the greatest effort. The nature of the sanction will depend on the circumstances of the individual institution. An institution which has decided to make itself largely dependent on international recruitment, either to fill places or generate income or both, may have done so because there is a shortfall in income from other areas. A decline in home numbers and inability to win research contracts, or the introduction of initiatives that can only be financed by the international income stream, may result in a real desire for international revenue. In general, the 'hungrier' the institution, the less need there is for sanctions. Survival, continued employment and participation in future expansion are all goals which, once explained by management, are easily understood at all levels. At the other end of the scale, well-resourced institutions that can attract the highest quality students and can afford to look after them when they are in the UK avoid some of the difficulties and see the enterprise in a more optimistic light.

The great majority are set somewhere between the two poles, with a strategic plan which encompasses gradual, well-planned growth in international numbers. There are many committed 'internationalists' among the academic community; there are also many diverse demands to be met and competing attractions for colleagues' time. When a new masters course or undergraduate option threatens to take time from the preparation of a journal article, when consultancy with industry may be more immediately rewarding than helping another research student to perfect his presentation in his second language, and where European Framework Programmes can be more seductive than exhibition participation after an eight-hour flight, then what is to persuade the colleague and the head of department that the 'international' call can be answered? Some institutions have looked at promotion criteria to see if international commitment can find a place with scholarship and teaching ability. Some have created posts of responsibility which reflect international commitment – either as student advisers or regional coordinators. Some have set up incentive schemes which transfer a percentage of the tuition fee to the department which attracts and registers the student. Some have redistributed the MASN so that key recruiting departments can increase their international recruitment and maintain the desired quota mix. The sensitivity required for such an approach is self-evident. As has been said, some institutions could consist of only law and management, while viking studies or musicology disappeared without trace. One institution in Australia relates its staff salaries partially to overseas recruitment, thus paying incentives directly into the admitting colleague's pocket. All these are positive sanctions and few institutions will discuss the other side of the coin. Some institutions with unsympathetic departments may decide to double monitor the admissions process and ask for full explanations of all rejected international applications. There comes a point for most individuals and departments when they require something of management. That may be promotion, or additional staffing before some initiative is undertaken, or support for a capital programme. Contribution to the plan for international recruitment may then be weighed in the balance.

Most colleagues face a heavy and increasing workload and expanding responsibility. The institution should persuade them to support the corporate international objective by information, discussions, negotiation and imagination. Real dialogue and a clear flow of information, together with immediate support if things go wrong, can encourage the least enthusiastic internationalist to work towards the corporate aim.

The institution now has a strategy expressed in a plan which identifies numbers of international students, the areas and the courses on which they may be registered, the level of study most appropriate for them and the effect that all this will have on the ethos of the whole. It has a budget forecast of expenditure and income and an organization to implement the plan. It has debated the plan at all levels through the proper mechanisms. It has accepted that certain inducements will be needed to ensure that the majority is convinced of the need to put real commitment into the meeting of the international aim, which for most institutions today is only one aim among many.

Delivery mechanisms

One final consideration should be debated. The issue of where and how the award-bearing courses are to be delivered has become increasingly important over the last five years, and is likely to become more so. The traditional and now simplistic view that to gain an award from X requires residence in X has been successfully questioned, and most institutions wishing to recruit post-16-year-olds are aware of, and usually have discussed, the complex factors involved. On a basic level, the plan should include some agreed view on distance learning, non-award-bearing students, short courses and other types of programme delivered off-site.

Opportunity and need

An institution, new either to international recruitment or to a particular market, should be cautious about taking any immediate steps into these non-traditional areas. There is no doubt, however, that options other than full-time attendance on main campus are becoming more popular. As the availability of technology has increased, so has the range of delivery mechanisms. Video conferencing, web access and interactive email have all encouraged institutions to consider whether the same quality outcome can be obtained by any one of a diversity of mechanisms. National desires to reduce the outflow of currency on education overseas and other more complex questions of cultural integrity have led some governments to review the benefits of supporting their brightest citizens to gain UK or other qualifications by three or four years of consecutive full-time study abroad.

Quality issues – the Codes

Such has been the speed of development, however, and the escalating rate of change in the arrangements that UK institutions have promoted or agreed to, that a number of quality and monitoring agencies have advocated caution and underlined the need for adherence to agreed criteria. The British Council, UKCOSA (United Kingdom Council for Overseas Affairs), the CVCP (Committee of Vice-Chancellors and Principals), the HEQC (Higher Education Quality Council) and, lately, Dearing, have all recommended that the institutions confine themselves to quality activities. This means quality that can be externally assessed as equal to that available to and required of regular students. This debate includes twinning, branch campuses, franchise degrees and other non-standard delivery packages. In this context, the National Committee of Inquiry into Higher Education, which reported in 1997, stated:

> We are particularly concerned to ensure that, when a programme is franchised by one institution to another, the standard required, and the quality of provision offered to the student, is no lower than in the parent institution. As the practice of franchising has expanded rapidly, we are concerned that some further education institutions may have extended themselves too broadly and entered into too many relationships. There have also been very small numbers of cases where control by UK higher education institutions of programmes franchised overseas has been inadequate. In the interests of extending opportunity and encouraging lifelong learning, franchising should continue, but only where quality assurance and the maintenance of standards are not prejudiced.
>
> (NCIHE 1997: 17)

Lord Dearing's Committee went on to recommend, 'after 2001, no franchising should take place either in the UK or abroad except where compliance with the criteria has been certified by the Quality Assurance Agency' (NCIHE 1997: Recommendation 23).

It may be helpful here to identify what is generally meant by 'franchise', which is often used loosely to cover a range of related activities. As the concepts were becoming more 'popular' and their implementation less rigorous, the HEQC circulated a document at the beginning of 1997. Its scope was wide and so clearly defined that it is worth quoting in full here.

The Scope of the Code

The Code is concerned with all arrangements entered into by UK universities and colleges with overseas universities, colleges, other providers of higher education, and public and private agencies, which involve one or more of the following:

- The award of a degree or other qualification of the UK institution;
- The provision by the overseas partner of all or part of a programme of study franchised to it by the UK institution;
- The provision of a programme of study designed and taught by an overseas institution, which has been approved or validated by a UK institution;
- Direct entry, or entry with advanced standing, of students to UK institutions by virtue of their satisfactory progress in approved programmes in an overseas partner institution;
- Preferential or non-preferential consideration of applicants to study at a UK institution by virtue of their satisfactory completion of a preparatory or foundation course provided by an overseas partner;
- The facilitation by an overseas partner of distance-learning programmes offered by UK institutions;
- Any other association which allows an overseas institution to use the name of a UK institution, or to refer to an award of that UK institution in any context.

Students (including research degree students) covered by the Code include non-UK students studying for UK awards in their own countries, and UK and non-UK students studying for UK awards on an approved course of study at an institution outside the UK.

(HEQC 1996: 3–4)

This, therefore, covers:

- the franchising of parts of UK-awarded qualifications;
- the validation of courses which form components of UK qualifications;
- the acceptance of overseas qualifications towards the final UK award (advanced standing);
- the incorporation of teaching in overseas institutions into the UK award.

It also includes provision for control of jointly supervised research degree programmes.

Quality issues – the difficulties

The Code requires the UK participant to look closely at its own motives for collaboration, and to recognize the likely motivation of the overseas partner. There is no doubt that the establishment of such agreements can lead to significant income flows and influence for the UK institution, as it can for the overseas collaborator. A proportion of the overseas partners will be private institutions or companies who, while sometimes being motivated by philanthropy or national pride, will also often have responsibility to their shareholders.

Quality in staffing, in facilities, in ongoing monitoring and audit is expensive to secure and maintain. Quality in student entry is even more expensive as it may require determination to work with smaller numbers and, therefore, to sacrifice some economies of scale and volume arrangements. These are difficult decisions and move the UK institution into a realm of property prices, international manpower planning, overseas legislation, depreciation of assets and opportunity costs, which at an earlier stage would have been unprecedented. The aim of the Code is – as was later reinforced by Dearing – to ensure that 'the standards of awards and programmes provided through partnerships with overseas institutions of Higher Education are comparable with those available at partner institutions within the UK' (HEQC 1996). While UK institutions of HE are the focus here, the principles laid down are broadly applicable to any educational institution. They can be applied, for example, to British schools being established in partnership in Thailand, to undergraduate courses shared with colleges in Malaysia, or to Australian distance learning programmes offered in Vietnam.

The dilemma is a constant and widely experienced one for the UK institution and these tensions have to be recognized and addressed before a valid plan can be published. In this aspect of international recruitment, more than any other, lies the opportunity to acquire short-term income at medium-term cost – and further long-term disaster. It must be understood that those most vulnerable are the students who may gain qualifications whose quality is tainted and, therefore, less marketable. The UK institutions are also at risk – and not only those participating in the collaboration. UK plc has been discussed in an earlier section. When the reputation of one UK institution is sullied, all suffer. The market may be tolerant, but it is not infinitely forgiving and the system will be compromised if isolated errors become regular debacles.

There is every good reason for all these partnership promotions in a world of finite resources. It is not surprising that the Malaysian government, for example, wishes to reduce expenditure on under-graduate overseas training. It is entirely understandable that the sponsors of mature PhD candidates from North Africa find the jointly supervised programme more appropriate for their needs. It is to be expected that those agencies charged with funding educational development across a country as large as Brazil will seek to spread their sponsorship among more students by reducing the length of individual overseas residence. It is also to be recognized that those institutions whose budgets are vulnerable to sudden reduction in overseas income will be seeking alternative methods of safeguarding cash flow and influence. The pattern of international education is dynamic. It offers potential for change to as great an extent as it does for home students. An increase in knowledge, experience and confidence will make for a greater acceptance of innovation in de-livery methods. The institutions are committed to achieving excel-lence, not to cherishing immutability. If the strategic planning can, therefore, give thought to the proper selection of partners and care-ful financial arrangements, then imaginative delivery and excellence at the point of exit are not mutually exclusive. These arrangements should be made under a formal agreement, which includes rigorous quality controls covering appointment of staff, design of curric-ulum, monitoring of systems, facilities and assessment. The institu-tion, however, must have researched the opportunity thoroughly before taking advantage of it, and have a sufficient level of resources and expertise to manage even a worst-case scenario. An institution unfamiliar with a country or inexperienced in international mar-keting is more likely to be faced with difficulties.

Quality issues – the dangers

The desire for, and the need to, enter into these partnership arrange-ments is accelerating the pace of change. At one time a foundation course, as an alternative to A Levels, was considered radical. The acceptance of these courses led to validation, or franchise, of first-year undergraduate programmes offered overseas. In recent years in the UK there has been a notable move towards acceptance of third-year undergraduate entry (known as 2 + 1) and a handful of institu-tions are now offering the whole of the degree programme overseas (3 + 0). At the same time, some of the most embarrassing of the UK educational exposés have centred upon the perceived lack of quality and rigour in such initiatives. Press articles like the following are widely read at home and overseas:

an unknown number of blank X examination certificates were distributed in Malaysia due to the institution's 'seriously flawed' overseas control arrangements . . . The report (from the National Audit Office) calls for funding council chiefs to encourage the Quality Assurance Agency to introduce a kite mark for meeting the high standards expected of British Higher Education.

(Tysome 1998)

Concern about the detrimental effects of sloppy, greedy and sub-standard arrangements is growing. 'Work is needed with the QAA to restore the credibility of British qualifications overseas. Franchising, which is clearly money led, and insufficiently rigorously controlled, should stop' (*Times Higher Education Supplement* 1998). If the decision is made to establish or expand an overseas collaboration, the institution needs to be particularly sensitive to all the issues of timing and resourcing covered in this chapter, as well as those of agents, marketing and student support considered in Chapters 3 and 4.

Short courses offered overseas

The less complicated offering of short courses off-site could also be considered when planning a portfolio of opportunities. Sometimes Ministries, universities or large employers overseas approach HE or FE institutions, inviting them to provide two- or three-week programmes – quite often at technical level, but occasionally requiring modules from masters programmes. It is generally understood that the overseas promoter will provide a venue and any equipment required, such as computers, together with advertising beforehand and support throughout the programme. The institution provides the speaker/s, the materials/intellectual property and the assessment procedures, if any are required, at the end of the period. A certificate of attendance or satisfactory progress may be given. It is sensible, if possible, to provide more than one institutional contributor as there can be substantial pressures on a solitary member of staff living in a hotel in a different culture. In addition, in such circumstances ill health, even for a day, threatens course completion. The financial responsibility for the hotel accommodation, subsistence, travel and even honorarium depends on whether the institution is simply assisting with the course or profit sharing. If the former, all expenses including honoraria or consultancy fees for staff are met by the overseas organizer. If the latter, the arrangements can be made according to level of fee charged to participants and the numbers expected.

Such schemes can afford institutions an opportunity to:

- develop relationships and network in the country in which they wish to market;
- meet students interested in the subject area who may eventually wish to progress onto full award-bearing courses abroad;
- expose staff to a cultural and academic system from which some of their existing full-time students may already come and from which more may in the future;
- generate income without responsibility for establishing infrastructures and systems.

Disadvantages arise if the numbers of staff likely to be involved are small. The responsibility becomes onerous if the partner organization is dilatory, neglectful or unscrupulous, and if the level of teaching does not match the institution's profile, if the financial arrangement proves inadequate or unrealistic and if the partner institution conducts itself in any way that is detrimental to the institution's reputation. The key to this, as with other non-standard delivery initiatives, lies in the selection of the overseas institution, in comprehensive discussions with the department concerned to ensure commitment and in a clear understanding from the institutional point of view of what can be gained from the collaboration. Minimal financial returns can be accepted if the collaboration provides opportunities for academic enrichment, positive introductions in the right areas and an inside track on high-quality student recruitment. The deal to avoid is one where key members of staff in an over-pressed department conduct a short course overseas, while the full-time students back home are being taught or supervised by colleagues 'bought in' for the purpose. An institution needs to be aware of the increasing trend towards non-standard delivery and of the safeguards which need to be invoked to protect all parties.

Conclusion

Strategic plans, however carefully debated and discussed, only remain valid for a limited period of time. There is a constant need for adaptation to changing circumstances. It is perhaps comforting for the heads of institutions beset by traditionalists on one side and pragmatists on the other to remember that universities have always been subject to these tensions. Rashdall wrote of them: 'University institutions must undergo perpetual modification in the future as they have undergone perpetual modification in the past' (Rashdall

1936).[10] They must be responsive, dynamic, and even pragmatic if they are to be credible in the changing fields of education, economics and politics – all of which have considerable influence on academic planning. While such key variables as the fluctuation of national currencies or foreign policy may influence tactics rather than strategy, they can affect some fundamental decisions. The Iran/Iraq war, the referendum which led to the inclusion of Finland in the European Union and the change in the Kenyan secondary school system all affected tactics and markets and, although disturbing at the time, were not critical. Something as significant as a return to the 'buy British last' policy in Malaysia or a decision by the Australian government to offer scholarships to all international students would certainly require a review of institutional direction in the UK. It is important, therefore, that strategy should be flexible in some areas – not in quality of the product but in the mix of the product range; not in commitment to the enterprise but in the pathways to the goal. Any strategy must be supported by contingency plans – the 'what if . . .' has to have the corollary 'then we can . . .'.

The elements which underpin the institution's plan for overseas recruitment are quite possibly those required for any other section of the plan:

- Can we afford it (have we the resources to do it to a high standard)?
- Is it appropriate (does it enhance the reputation and accord with the goals of the institution)?
- Can we deliver it (do we have the skills and knowledge) and will it attract sufficient commitment from all those involved in making it work?
- Are we sufficiently independent of it (does it provide only that proportion of income whose loss will not threaten the institution's existence)?

If the answers to all the above are positive, then the institution can look with some confidence to the next layer of decision making – the tactics by which success can be achieved.

Endnotes

1 Peat Marwick, Management Consultants, also wrote (1986: 38): 'The Jarratt report identified planning and use of resources as the area where the universities have the greatest opportunity to improve their efficiency and effectiveness.'

2 MASN is the number agreed by government as the full-time home undergraduate intake figure for HE. If the MASN is exceeded beyond the error margin, the institution is required to pay a penalty. Dearing described this as follows: 'After a very rapid rise in the number of students between 1988 and 1993, the Government placed a cap on any further growth in publicly-funded full time undergraduate student numbers' (NCIHE 1997: Summary, 11). His report recommended to the government 'that it should have a long term strategic aim of responding to increased demand for higher education, . . . and that to this end, the cap on full time undergraduate places should be lifted over the next two or three years' (Recommendation 1).

3 A Levels (or Advanced Levels) are completed at the age of 18 years after 13 years of study and the GCSE (formerly O Level) at the age of 16 years after 11 years of study. Both are nationally validated examinations and assessments in the UK.

4 The IB Diploma programme is a two-year pre-university course designed to facilitate the mobility of students, promote international understanding and provide a widely accepted university matriculation qualification. The subject marking is graded on a scale of 1 to 7 and the award of the Diploma requires a minimum total of 24 points. One subject must be offered in each of the six groups and at least three must be offered at higher level – the remainder at subsidiary level.

5 If students are admitted to foundation courses in institutions of FE, it seems that a UCAS application is not required on entry to the course but can be completed during the Foundation period. If students seek admission to a foundation course offered at an institution of HE, they are frequently required to complete the full UCAS procedures prior to entry.

6 The MBA programme, for example, will recruit students from a wide range of first degree disciplines. An MA or MSc in Information Technology may be seen as a conversion programme in a similar way.

7 Research Council support and recognition may require that only a limited proportion of the credits can be gained from first degree or Diploma modules.

8 The financial implications of the RAE have to be considered as well as the academic issues. Many of the leading UK institutions will now have plans whose policies focus on their inclusion as research leaders in the next RAE. They would aspire to ratings of Grade 4 and above in the majority of disciplines. Grades 4, 5 and 5* indicate that the subject areas assessed are in part or in whole centres of international activity.

9 CONACYT (Consejo Nacional de Ciencia y Tecnologia) is one of the key national funding agencies in Brazil as is YÖK (the Higher Education Council) in Turkey.

10 Dearing re-emphasized this with the view that 'External factors have affected the development of higher education since the Robbins report . . . in the early 1960s. We judge that external changes will be even more influential over the next 20 years' (NCIHE 1997: Summary, 12).

3

SELLING THE PRODUCT: DECIDING ON AND IMPLEMENTING INSTITUTIONAL TACTICS

Introduction

There are over 190 self-governing countries in the world. Any institution interested in international recruitment must have a policy for reviewing each of them, categorizing them by applying criteria already discussed and deciding which to select for market penetration. There is not an institution in the United Kingdom or in any advanced industrial nation which has a budget large enough to finance a proactive campaign in every country, nor sufficient time to spend in exploring at first hand each of the 'possible' nations. It is, therefore, essential that as a key tactic in its operational plan, the institution should investigate the potential of each market and then decide where and how to focus its effort.

Defining a recruitment market

The period spent in study overseas is usually an interlude between education in the student's home country and a return to that country for employment. The institution promoting the study in its country must, therefore, be knowledgeable about the education system from which the student has come and the local economy and employment opportunities to which he or she will return.

Educational system

Most countries will have some international schools which allow only a very small minority of indigenous students to follow a programme leading to International General Certificate of Secondary Education (IGCSE), Advanced Levels (A Level), the International Baccalaureate (IB) or Scholastic Aptitude Tests (SATs) and Advanced Placement Tests (APTs) [1] In most cases, such international schools were primarily established for expatriate children and few of the local population could enrol. Only a very small number of the indigenous population will choose to come for secondary schooling overseas, and so the vast majority with aspirations for further and higher education overseas will be educated through the local secondary system. In deciding on which countries to focus attention, the quality of the local system is a key consideration.

- What is the school leaving qualification?
- What is its standard and content?
- What is the breadth of subjects covered and, consequently, how much depth can be expected?
- At what age do the students leave school and at what age and for how long do they attend local universities to graduate with a first degree?
- How secure and reliable is the assessment procedure and how valid as a national yardstick of intellectual ability and attainment?
- How much trust can be placed in the documentation?
- How much knowledge is there of, for example, the UCAS system?
- How much likelihood is there of gaining a school report?

These questions are just the beginning of any survey and relate only to admission to further education or undergraduate study.

If postgraduate courses are to recruit, then the overseas institutions must know the level and quality of the local first degree, any qualifications which might be regarded as equivalent to a first degree, the manner of grading the first degree and the reliability or indeed availability of references. When deciding on the acceptability of a market for undergraduate study, the host institution must decide whether it could safely admit directly to the first year of an undergraduate course or would require access via, for example, A Levels or IB or a foundation programme. The various advantages and disadvantages of these routes have been discussed in the preceding chapter. If A Levels are the desired route, then the UK institution will have to understand that all its marketing activity will result in increased numbers of students at UK schools and colleges in preparation for admission to an institution of higher education. Is trawling for undergraduates, therefore, worth the effort, or would a better use of resources involve close liaison and joint marketing with selected schools and colleges in the UK? If a foundation course is to be suggested, then consideration should be given as to whether this is taught in or out of the host institution's premises, whether it is free-standing or tied, accredited or simply accepted. Some foundation courses require commitment by the student on registration to a single institution; others will place students in a variety of institutions depending on student wishes and level of achievement. The former offers a degree of security and early integration, the latter the same freedom of choice enjoyed by any UCAS candidate. A further choice which involves sharing the degree programme with a local institution (often known as twinning) has proved a popular option in some countries for some institutions. This option has been discussed in the preceding chapter.

Graduate programmes at individual overseas universities can be even harder to assess and evaluate. The various levels of institutions need to be understood. Some countries have a mixture of junior colleges, universities, polytechnics, three-year colleges and specialized institutions. It is necessary to understand the academic quality of the awards given by all of these to produce a market analysis. Degrees are classified in a variety of ways. Some conform easily to the honours and class of degree system, others offer alphabetical transcripts, percentage-based assessments or cumulative Grade Point Average (GPA).[2] The absence of an external examiner system may lead some institutions to be uncertain of the comparability of institutions one with another. If the country sustains systems of national, municipal, state and private universities, a full knowledge will be required of the strengths of each of these. As in the UK, the quality of departments may well vary in the same institution. To complicate a difficult situation yet further, overriding political considerations may apply. In every country in the world, a university will bring together imaginative, articulate, idealistic and talented young people and governments can expect them to be centres of intellectual ferment as well as education. Some countries will therefore experience periods of university disruption, unrest, repression and closure. Students coming out of them may, therefore, have suffered disruption of their studies and may have been unable to achieve their potential level of performance. These are some of the factors that affect market suitability as it relates to the educational system and will need to be taken into account.

Facility in English language

This is a key consideration for English language-medium institutions for obvious reasons. English may well be counted as one of the three world languages of the twenty-first century but there is still a large number of overseas countries where its use is limited and its mastery difficult. Even those countries that regard English as the second language have a wide range of competence in acquiring it. Fluency in English, as a widespread national phenomenon, brings in its train a knowledge of English culture, products and literature. Such a market may already have turned towards the UK for commerce, or services, or leisure and will be predisposed to look towards it for education. It may even teach at secondary or tertiary level in the medium of English. Facility in English, however, is not always an indication of a market with assured potential. English is also the language of the USA, Canada, Australia and New Zealand and, as has been discussed in the opening chapters, these can be regarded by the UK to some extent as 'competitor' nations.

Social, cultural and political factors

The need for assistance with interpretation of systems and qualifications is emphasized in Chapter 5. Cultural, financial and political considerations will effect market suitability. If a country is open to 'internationalization', it is likely to value and seek the opportunity for its young people to study overseas. If a country has a government hostile to the recruiting country it is unlikely to assist its students to live there. If the political, social or religious systems and conventions of the host country are seen as dangerous, seductive or corrupt by another country's government or people, then there will be little wish to gain their credentials. If the country is impoverished, with little spare public spending power, or without a middle class – however small – with disposable income, then the opportunity for successful recruitment may be limited. If, however, in these circumstances the recruiting institution is confident of its ability to attract major aid funding or is in a position to offer scholarships of its own then the marketing possibilities are considerable. A discussion on scholarship funding can be found in Chapter 5. The need to differentiate markets and assess their potential has been understood since full-fee marketing began in the UK in the early 1980s. The first three localities for the new British Council ECS service in 1984 were Malaysia, Hong Kong and Singapore and these choices were easily justifiable. All of them had educational systems that in the main fed easily into undergraduate programmes in the UK. Students with A Level and STPM[3] qualifications moved smoothly into first-year degrees. Indeed, at one point it was argued that Hong Kong A Level grades were worth one grade higher than their UK equivalents. As the UK selectors became more sophisticated and better informed, they were able to make judgements on second-year entry for certain polytechnic diploma holders. FE, too, has had an opportunity to recruit from pre-A Level candidates for courses leading to university entry or vocation qualifications. Understanding was gained of the teacher training qualifications in Hong Kong which enabled UK institutions to create a route to the Bachelor of Education (BEd). In these countries, as the British Council was aware, was a facility with the English language and an affection for, or at least a longstanding knowledge of, things British. Many of the middle-class parents from these countries who sent their children to study in the UK had themselves benefited from a British education. Indeed, in Malaysia this applied not just to the expanding middle class but also to the members of the royal family whom UK institutions are proud to claim as alumni. The political stability of these countries and their economic success, together with government policies that were broadly in line with the UK philosophies, made them ideal recipients of UK marketing. The significance attached to the choice of language was evidenced by the changing dictates of government concerning learning in the medium of English. There were several changes in the system in Malaysia during the 1980s. The economic difficulties which developed in South East Asia at the time of writing will lead institutions to review and analyse their recruitment policies. They will be compelled to confront their motivation for and commitment to international recruitment. Malaysia, Singapore and Hong Kong are not among the largest countries, nor have the biggest populations in the world. They were, however, for all the reasons explained above, the first examples of successful UK marketing and continue to provide some of the largest national groups of students in the UK.

At the other end of the spectrum, Latin America, Myanmar, Laos, Cambodia, Vietnam, the Middle East and the former Soviet nations remained more difficult to interest. Some had school systems which proved opaque, others a traditional affinity with the USA, others political philosophies which discouraged international education, or citizens with only subsistence-level incomes. With an increase of knowledge and experience on the UK side and changes within the countries themselves, growing success has been experienced in recruiting from them. The natural corollary of this, student exchange and credit transfer, will be discussed in the concluding chapter.

Researching a market

If these are the criteria by which markets are judged as suitable for recruitment initiatives, then the next consideration must be the mechanism for establishing the facts on which to assess the criteria. The institution, unless it has a very favourable budget, will want to access and examine detailed information available at home before it makes its first sortie abroad. While all the following is available in hard copy, the advent of the web and internet has led to even easier collection of information. The possibility of confusion through an over-abundance of web information should be taken seriously! General knowledge and newspaper reading supplemented by periodicals like the *Economist* provide digestible background information on the current state of the country in question and the difficulties or opportunities facing it. Learned journals, such as *Nature*, may provide an assessment of the state of a particular academic discipline in the country or an institution within it. A spate of articles on the environment, a conference on pollution with publications on sewage disposal problems may give an indication of interest in that area. A country at the point of expanding its tourist industry may be ready to look for graduate courses in hotel management, food process management or leisure development. It may also be looking in the shorter term for English language programmes.

The British Council market surveys have, over the last ten years, proved themselves to be excellent reference points. They offer information gathered in-country and assessed by an experienced consultant or practitioner.[4] It is not suggested that they can identify exactly which institution's portfolio could be well received in the overseas market, but they can and do identify sectors which might be successful and recommend ways by which success may be achieved. So far all these measures can be taken at the desk with negligible expenditure and with no public commitment. Life being as it is, luck, chance, opportunity can all play a part and the decision to 'go with it' when the chance occurs is less hazardous if it can be supported as well on grounds of market research already prudently undertaken. A colleague may have attended an overseas conference and met an academic from X who sees potential in research collaboration. An alumnus, maybe from 50 years ago, suddenly comes to local prominence. A visitor, perhaps one of many in a busy month, by chance meets the right colleague or recognizes a uniquely appropriate facility. A newly appointed member of staff has been born and educated abroad and has the language, enthusiasm and connections to develop something in his or her own country. You fall into conversation on a long plane flight and possibilities for collaboration emerge at 33,000 feet! All of these examples are real ones. Some or all of them must occur regularly. The institution may fail to hear about them, may fail to recognize them, may wish to develop them but have too limited a budget to resource them. It may debate the opportunity and, after well-informed discussion, decide not to pursue it for all or any of the reasons identified in Chapter 2. This is the proper use of the strategic plan. It is impossible to believe that any institution will have the resources and the energy to follow through every opportunity. Failure of communication, recognition or resources are all discussed later in the book. Success or failure in developing the market once it has been identified as appropriate are the subject of the sections which follow.

The final mechanism for market selection is the visit and, as the most expensive of the market research activities, it should be kept to the end and planned carefully. In some cases, a visit to analyse the market is not necessary – the data and advice obtained has been comprehensive. In some cases, too, the research visit can be combined with a recruitment activity or at least an event to raise awareness. Expensive and time-consuming it may be but it remains generally agreed that nothing carries as much immediate impact as personal contact. The chance to experience at first hand student quality and the system and environment from which potential students will come is sure to add to the strength of the recruitment drive. If it is well planned and conducted with sensitivity it should also provide the opportunity to establish friendly relations with colleagues and officials who will be key to the success of future efforts in that region.

Penetrating a market

A decision has now been reached on the basis of all of the above that Never Never Land will be a country where effective work could be repaid. When discussing budgets and financial planning there will be a consideration of the differences between countries which are to be targeted as a focus for recruitment and those where the existing presence can only be maintained, and the consequent extent of expenditure on each of the two groups.

Mail shot

The mail shot allows literature to arrive in the selected country quickly and at low cost. It is a desk-based operation that can be highly effective – or a complete waste of time and money if the destination or the content of the shot results in its consignment to the bin.

Logistics

A successful mail shot has found the correct answers to the questions, 'who', 'what', 'when' and 'how'? The question 'why?' should have been cleared in the strategic plan before the mail shot was considered. 'Who?' means the identification of the ultimate recipient – or more likely the person who will have in-country access to the intended recipient. The 'ultimate recipients' in a secondary school will be the individual students and their parents, but the vehicle will often be the careers counsellor or the head teacher. If post-graduates are being sought then the head of a university department or a contact in a sponsoring organization, such as a Ministry, may be the channel of communication. If short course English language students are the ultimate target then the heads of language schools may be appropriate contacts. It is at this point that the process becomes circular and success builds on success. If the schools have already been visited and contact made with the head teacher or counsellor, then the letter can be precisely addressed and contain some personal warmth. If talks have already been held with sponsors, then the letter and details can reflect these discussions. Every contact, however, has to be initiated somewhere and the mail shot, if implemented thoughtfully, can be a very effective means of 'cold calling'. The British Council will supply lists of school and university addresses and, where additional details are required, the Embassy or High Commission in London or the UK Embassies overseas can be helpful. Such mailing lists will rarely indicate a named recipient – usually only a title.

The logistics of the mailing list and the mail shot, once agreed upon, are usually left to the least senior member of staff in the office. A simple sum to calculate the postage, time and materials expended on a wasted mail shot should encourage those ultimately responsible for its success to explain its importance carefully to those addressing or filling the envelopes. The whole issue of communication and commitment is considered in later chapters. The increased use of information technology has revolutionized systems, and databases and mail merge can now create a far more effective and efficient distribution. However, it still requires someone to sort the mailing list and update it as necessary. A mailing list jumble of secondary schools and universities with contacts met at conferences, British Council personnel, eager alumni and Ministry officials is a negative asset.

Contents and timing

It should go without saying that there is a correlation between who is to be mailed and what is to be enclosed. The contents of the shot require some careful research of the market. It is, for instance, an indication of ignorance of the system – and a sure waste of effort – if foundation course material is sent to schools preparing candidates for A Level or IB, or from whom directly admitted students are sought. It is not helpful, on the other hand, if schools offering the Kenyan Certificate of Secondary Education (KCSE)[5] are offered only undergraduate details without mention of access routes. It is not helpful, for example, to send a mail shot to Cypriot schools without reference to the acceptability of the Apolytirion. It is a wasted opportunity if Japanese universities are sent only full undergraduate course details when one-semester packages of study abroad could also be offered. It could be meaningless to send post-experience Masters course literature to new graduates, or to send summer school language programmes to candidates whose summer vacation does not coincide with that of the host institution. There will obviously be exceptions to all of these 'rules' – they are only intended to emphasize the need for relevant knowledge to be gained and thought given to the shot before the envelopes are filled.

Once the appropriate literature has been identified, the advantages of a covering letter are clear. Attention can be drawn to the salient points in the documents. Details can be given of the existing or past students' successes and numbers. The beginnings of a personal relationship can be forged so that the host institution can establish a point of contact. The timing of the shot is also important. Holiday periods may or may not be suitable, examination periods may need to be avoided if maximum impact is to be gained. Some school systems encourage early UCAS choice and completion. Some sponsors have scholarships available at the end of their financial year. Some language schools require regular mailings and updating. Some countries have a lengthy lead-in time for visas which mean that early decisions on departures push back the date for the application and consequently that for promotional material. Any mail shot that does not enclose extra documentation should now be considered for email distribution and the coding of mailing addresses should be held in emailed bookmarks. Soon, when almost all an institution's public documents are on the web, many countries will be able to call them down, read them and apply electronically. In some countries the internet is forbidden, in some it is not available and for several years to come it will be a tool which is not equally available to all potential students in all regions. The airmail

envelope has not yet come to the end of its useful life but its days as
the prime instrument for communication are numbered.

If the institution's central budget bears the cost of mail shots overseas there is less urgent need for those initiating them to analyse the
cost-effectiveness of every shot. When budgets are decentralized and
the exact cost of airmailing a glossy prospectus is calculated as part
of the section budget then it may be reviewed more rigorously. The
mail shot carefully organized, supervised and evaluated continues to
be a useful tool in the armoury of profile raising and information
distribution. Behind it, of course, looms the larger question of the
institution's corporate image as expressed in every piece of literature it produces from the covering letter to the course details, the
application form and the envelope. This is basic to any marketing –
at home as well as overseas.

Advertisements

Let us assume that the UK institution has now made use of information relating to the market and has distributed details of its products
as widely and judiciously as possible within the selected country.
A demand is identified and the institution wishes to fill it. With
almost every post there comes an invitation to place advertisements
and to attend exhibitions. Both of these activities are expensive
and both can be counterproductive and extravagant unless handled
properly both before and after the event. Both are seductive in the
opportunities to which they allude.[6] The call to advertise may conceal
pitfalls similar to bulk mailing – unless the message is appropriate,
the audience targeted and the response evaluated, it can prove an
expensive mistake. Advertisements cannot list all the courses and
facilities at any institution, but they can prompt interest and elicit
enquiries. Sometimes a section of the institution may choose to
advertise alone or in collaboration with others. Sometimes the institution wishes to give a corporate picture. If advertisements are to raise
general profile they must be shaped by a desire for a specific outcome.
If they are to elicit enquiries, there must be an effective system in
place to respond to them. There must be some understanding, too,
of the status of the reader. It would be unusual if postgraduate research candidates were attracted from advertisements placed in maga-
zines read by secondary school students, or that interest in foundation
courses would flow from advertisements placed in scientific journals.
The productivity of advertisements can be evaluated if a question is
included on course application forms as to where the information was
first accessed. Such evaluation is also made easier if advertisements

carry 'coded' addresses such as 'Room 23', which instantly identifies source. Never underestimate the germination time of advertisements and brochures – enquiries have been known to straggle in several years after the last appearance of either!

Exhibitions

History and value

There can be scarcely anyone involved in international recruitment who does not have his or her own tale of an overseas exhibition. They were the first large public activity organized through the British Council Education Counselling Service and were for many institutions the first route into in-country marketing. For some they remain the only route. In the glory days of the early 1980s international students flocked to the spectacle of British representatives available to talk about courses, advise on entry standards, distribute many tons of glossy literature and genuinely and generally present the acceptable face of UK further and higher education. That has been the overriding motivation behind the exhibition phenomenon – to provide the opportunity for parents, students and sponsors to acquire not only the appropriate literature and advice but also to see and meet the people whom the institutions believe can best represent their image and ethos. Exhibitions have proved popular both with the potential applicants and the UK institutions. They are popular, too, with the organizers and stand erectors, the stand designers, the freight handlers, the tour companies and the airlines. They fulfil a serious marketing function. They also generate healthy incomes for the commercial services that come under their umbrella. That is not a criticism – mail shots help the stationery companies. It is, however, a warning that not every invitation to participate in an exhibition is based on market research that leads the organizer to believe that any individual institution will be well served by attendance. The good professional organizers, which group must include the British Council, realize that repeat orders for exhibition places are only obtained if those who attend are satisfied by the turnout that the exhibition produces – both in terms of volume and quality.

British Council and commercial exhibitions

The British Council runs exhibitions in a growing number of countries annually or biannually.[7] All ECS countries organize exhibitions, as do other British Council offices. These began as general exhibitions with all institutions in membership invited on a first response, first acceptance principle. They have branched into additional areas divided by sector or subject. There are now FE exhibitions, postgraduate exhibitions, art and design exhibitions and business and management exhibitions. There are clubs and consortia and groupings. The main guidelines of the British Council exhibition is that only British institutions can participate and that participation is governed by a Code of Conduct.[8] That Code can and does carry sanctions. It is expected that participants will behave in a professional manner, consistent with the integrity and dignity of their institutions. British Council venues and arrangements are intended to reflect the quality of the product they are displaying. British Council organized exhibitions are not part of any multinational exhibition but can join forces with UK trade and industry to present a broadly based British image. One of the largest of these was in Hong Kong at the end of the 1980s. For all these reasons they are not the cheapest in the market but it is generally accepted that the British Council logo will give the imprimatur to national quality and recognition.

In some countries at some times commercial agencies have arranged exhibitions before the British Council decided to do so or instead of the British Council or in collaboration with the British Council. Commercial organizations, often to maximize visitor numbers or income, may invite several nations to participate. It can be argued that the students have the advantage of being able to see their own institutions of higher education exhibiting at the same venue as those from Australia, New Zealand, Canada, the USA and the UK. Quite often there are no rules for institutional admission – accredited or non-accredited institutions may participate – and the student can exercise his or her judgement and discretion. This is a genuine case of caveat emptor, and perhaps a real risk when something as important and expensive as higher education is at stake. These exhibitions tend to be busier, livelier and noisier than the 'UK alone' variety. Some institutions complain that a student searching for an institution of excellence for his or her PhD studies can be seduced by the colour video of Vancouver or the give-away teddy koala. Others are delighted that students bound for a destination on the Pacific Rim have become interested in foundation courses in the UK Midlands. UK exhibitors' opinion is varied but the balance seems to be tipped in favour of UK alone events.

Organizing the stand

The exhibition, too, has come of age since the early 1980s. When notice of the exhibition was enough in itself to draw an interested crowd, very little else needed to be provided. Stand shell design gradually became an art in its own right furnished with collapsible stands, banners, wallpapers, tablecloths, give-aways, carrier bags, video loops and spotlighting. Each of these has relevance and can be seen as part of the composite image. Each institution has to decide how it wishes to be seen, conscious that the medium may be taken as the message. Practical considerations of cost, time and skill required to set up the stand and the stamina required to convey it have also to be borne in mind. Institutions with more limited budgets may not be able to provide pictures of appropriate student faces for every destination – one representative set of pictures may be all that is available. Care must then be taken to ensure that these do not carry any unintended messages. Muslim countries will not be so comfortable with pictures of young people of both sexes lying on the campus grass enjoying the sunshine together, or raising a tankard at the Union Bar. Images of dreaming spires and ivy-clad Halls may convey an image of the Britain of a bygone era unless there are also images of high-technology laboratories and cutting-edge research. 'Cool Britannia' is changing all this! Unless students have come purposely to a specific institution's stand, in which case the battle is halfway won, the image projected in that fleeting moment as he or she walks past is the one that will lead the student to stay and ask questions. Stand decoration is therefore vital. It should be attractive, simple and informative. Students like to see a map of the UK showing the institution's location and some basic detail such as programmes offered. They cannot read a mass of small print as they walk by but a single image can arrest their attention. If faces depicting a mixture of races are shown, it is as well to have a good idea of the 'acceptable mix' in that country. Similarly, it is not always appealing to show groups of international students alone together. Most international students have deliberately chosen to go overseas in order to become part of another culture, at least temporarily. Pictures of home and overseas students studying, living and relaxing together epitomize this vision.

Exhibition organizers provide furniture and fitments and the layout of these is dictated by the particular image that the institution wishes to promote, the physical shape of the venue and the volume of visitors. If hundreds of thousands of visitors are expected, the majority of whom will in effect collect paper, then a desk across the front of the stand can stop, or at least limit, access to the supplies of material. If a less frenetic exhibition is expected with discriminating students coming through in manageable numbers, then an open front with grouped seating will allow counselling and conversation. Most exhibitions fall somewhere between these extremes. Having attracted the interested visitor to the stand, the institution has two key means of information delivery. The first is the literature and the second is the personnel. The costs of sending both have to be considered, as does the best method of exploiting these resources and their suitability for the task in hand.

Participants – conduct

Psychologists, marketing consultants and common sense have all provided advice to those looking after exhibition stands. In addition to the obvious guidelines dictated by professionalism and common courtesy, there are a few that relate to the particular mores of the country in which the exhibition is sited. It is a mistake for any exhibitor to dress too casually. Many of the more traditional markets perceive dress and style as an indication of dignity, sobriety and integrity. This does not mean that the large number of younger visitors seeking FE or undergraduate entry will expect UK representatives to be pinstriped or dressed in boring and out-of-date clothes. It does mean that a considerable amount of money is being expended by families or sponsors on the education package and when they come to the exhibition they expect to meet someone who looks as though he or she is 'together'. In some countries low necklines on women, very short skirts or very high-cut sleeves will be regarded as inappropriate dress. Usually exhibition guidelines will bring this to exhibitors' attention. The matter of exhibition 'skills' has been discussed at length in a number of manuals. It is sufficient to say here that whether the exhibitor sits or stands at the entrance, says 'can I help you' or 'good morning' is of less importance than the fact that he or she is not consuming a heavy meal on view, is not lost in marking scripts or in a novel, looks and sounds welcoming and non-threatening and knows enough about the institution to add value to the brochures. As mentioned earlier, the representatives on the stand are expected to relay the institutional ethos. In a real sense, their institution will be judged initially by their conduct. If they are considerate, informative and courteous people, the enquirer will leave with a positive impression. Whether he or she later applies to that institution is a secondary concern here. The fact that the institution has given a good impression rather than a hard sales pitch is far more important. The idea of UK plc, to which reference is made on several occasions throughout this book, is paramount during exhibition times. Many enquirers will be aware that there are variations in quality between teaching and research in the various institutions. Others will be completely unaware that resources and specialisms are not uniform. Most exhibitors will have been faced with the statements, 'I have been offered a place for a PhD at X, would it be better to apply to you?' or 'My son hasn't put your institution on his UCAS form and he now has six offers, can he come to you?' or 'I really want to study serious science but you only offer serious engineering. Will it cover the same ground and are you among the national leaders?' The one comforting thought as you tread carefully through the minefield that surrounds these questions and their answers is that, on most occasions, decency and honesty also make practical and commercial good sense. The ratings are in the public domain[9] but they can be placed in context. Some research groups in these highly graded departments may be more suitable than some others in top-grade departments in which only a proportion of the staff have been entered into the RAE. The student's level of language and awareness of the complexities of the system will dictate how sophisticated the discussion should be.

It is never helpful to the student or to the UK system to indicate that a qualification from any UK university is not a commodity worth having. The rules of UCAS must be known by anyone representing the UK system. Many exhibitions now include a representative of UCAS from whom advice, confirmation of standing and data can be sought. While the UCAS system is in operation and includes overseas candidates, its rules should apply to prevent a descent into anarchy. Unless the most fundamental problems are revealed by the student, such as inability to pay fees without scholarships or radical new information about the student's personal life, it is inadvisable to suggest or encourage any last-minute changes of allegiance. Students and sponsors often know at postgraduate level the exact area of research specialism which attracts them. It is less than professional to claim expertise where the institution has none, to persuade into an allied area, or to claim total lack of knowledge of where it is available. No one institution can provide excellence in every specialism, or indeed even offer that specialism. Helpful guidance as to the institutions that do offer what is required and their location in the exhibition, or address if they are not present, would seem a professional response.

Participants – briefing

One of the several benefits that flow from a policy of distributing exhibition travel so as to include other colleagues in these activities is that new representatives are brought into play at regular intervals. The institution cannot expect that an academic with a heavy responsibility for teaching and research in his or her own subject will possess all the information on entry levels to other subjects, fees and scholarships, residential accommodation costs and a host of other important details. It is the responsibility of those organizing international recruitment to provide packages of information for new exhibitors and to accompany them with a briefing, together with a commitment to a debriefing. Such a briefing should include notes on how to take particulars, the details of agents or representatives in the field, on the make-up of the exhibition team and of any country update available. If the institutions have other current activities in that country these should be cross-referenced. There can be little more embarrassing for representatives than to be asked by an enquirer about the twinning scheme of their institution with a local college when they are not aware that one exists. Exhibitions are staffed according to need and resources available and often only one person will be asked to attend. The demands on that person are heavy but the camaraderie evident among the exhibitors at these events eases the burden on the sole participant and makes the task viable, even if exhausting.

Alumni assistance

Once the market potential for a country has been assessed and an exhibition arranged as a marketing mechanism, it is a mistake to view that exhibition attendance in isolation. Time-consuming and wearying as exhibitions can be, they should be seen as only a part of a package of initiatives. At the same time, one or two schools could be visited, alumni contacted, potential candidates telephoned and British Council staff met. If more than one colleague is attending, it is valuable to arrange stand schedules so that advantage can be taken of every visiting opportunity. The institution that must attend with only one delegate can often arrange to have alumni on the stand and all institutions benefit from the presence of articulate, satisfied past students. They are among the best of ambassadors and draw enquirers to the stand, reassure those who have already made a contact and inform and interest those who are at the point of decision. It is understandable that the parents of an 18-year-old who has never been out of the country before will gain comfort and confidence from the presence of compatriot graduates who went to the institution, enjoyed it, succeeded in the programme and who have returned to make a contribution to the country. The fact that alumni can offer this encouragement in their own language is a real bonus.

Like everything else in marketing, careful planning ensures greater success. Work with alumni is detailed in a later chapter but the arrival of the appropriate alumni on the stand is hardly ever achieved by mere good fortune. There are a few occasions, too, where monitoring is required. Those who left the institution 20 years ago will not necessarily know of the expanded range of courses, or the new School of X, or the foundation route, or the successful centre for pre-sessional English teaching, or the enlarged facility for family housing. They are even less likely to have heard of the indoor swimming pool or the research rankings or the new welcome programme. Few will know how many students from that country are currently studying in the UK institution. It is, therefore, the responsibility of the representative running the stand to brief alumni properly, to integrate them into the exhibition package and to deploy them to best advantage. They should not be left to work through an undergraduate prospectus in response to specific academic queries but rather treated as a resource and an advertisement.

Selecting and using the literature

Stand representatives and their literature should form a harmonious team, each complementing the other. The person responsible for the exhibition planning should know the market in that country well enough to pack appropriate freight. This is not an exact science. Over a three-day exhibition it is impossible to calculate precisely the right quantities of everything. It is, however, inexcusable if the exhibition in, for instance, Japan does not have a supply of study abroad, English language courses and foundation programme literature if the institution offers these. It would be equally remiss to arrive in Thailand without large numbers of postgraduate prospectuses if such courses are on offer. A decision has to be reached on the level of detail that is to be freighted and deployed. There are many successful strategies here and the institution must decide on the most appropriate for its own needs. It is good marketing, however, for the institution to have made a conscious decision and to understand the advantages and disadvantages of the way it chooses to operate in each context. It is possible to arrive with just one copy of the key composite brochure, usually a prospectus, and to counsel each student referring only to that document. Such an approach will require a very well-informed and totally committed exhibitor, as well as sticky labels or a laptop and a dedicated follow-up service. At the other end of the spectrum prospectuses, course brochures, generic leaflets are available in large quantities, together with preliminary enquiry forms. These are distributed liberally with an agreed amount allocated for each day. Somewhere in the middle is the stand with both ease of distribution and opportunity for conversation. Only the top 20 courses on this stand have literature available beyond the prospectus. Ideally, a generalist marketer fronts up the stand and takes notes of further information required. He or she answers questions on everything except detailed course specifics. A well-informed academic talks to students referred from the front who want discussion on content of courses and research programmes. Everyone with even a slight interest completes a data sheet which is either carried back home or input during the visit on the laptop. Any institution which can consistently achieve all the arrangements they desire is both skilled and lucky. The most promising manufacturing engineering PhD applicant will sometimes only be available when the engineering colleague is away from the stand visiting an institution. The one alumnus to gain a First in Music has just left the stand for home when the potential Music student arrives with his family. One institution with a carefully boxed set of completed enquiry forms lost them all in the rush for literature.

Interpreters

The debate on the use of interpreters and mother tongue literature continues. Once again, if interpreters are well briefed, well organized and integrated into the whole stand team much will be gained. In some cases they provide the only way of satisfactory communication. English-medium institutions, however, wish to attract to their academic courses students who already possess a high level of English language competence, or who are at least able to achieve that competence within a short time. If a student is completely incapable of communication in English it is unlikely that he or she will register on an award-bearing programme in that country in the middle-term future. Of course, if students are applying for language-only courses they can be expected to have a lower language level and interpreters or mother tongue literature are then essential. The presence of interpreters and vernacular literature, too, is most useful for sponsors and families. Very often undergraduates are accompanied by their parents or extended family, and postgraduates by their families. It is not to be expected that relatives will always be able to converse, or to understand the important details of housing and financial matters explained in English. It is even less likely that the British exhibitor will speak the local language. Some mother tongue literature or a banner on the exhibition stand, together with an interpreter, is an expression of a wish to communicate and an acknowledgement that most UK participants are at best only bilingual in certain modern European languages. The interpreter, like the alumnus, will also add reassurance and be able to tackle the more complex or sensitive questions.

A badly managed interpreter, however, can act as an impediment, blocking interaction between enquirer and representative. The interpreter can begin a conversation of his or her own, suggesting rather than interpreting, or, in the worst cases, can interpret inaccurately. Often the exhibitor needs to hear the applicants speak English and should encourage them to try. In many countries the level of 'passive' English language is much higher than that of 'active' language and the culture would lead the reserved student to seek an interpreter if one was available. Much of the rewarding and informative interchange with students is lost if interpreters are widely used. There will, of course, be occasions when communication fails, or is less than satisfactory, and at these times the availability of translation is vital. Perhaps the best arrangement is a well-managed alumni presence with a skilled professional interpreter available from a central source. One of the requirements of some exhibitions is that the stand should be manned by at least one person based in the host institutions. The requirements for this condition and the discussion of its implications will consider the whole wide-ranging and fraught questions of agents and representatives. Once again, if they are managed judiciously as part of the total package, their inclusion in the exhibition team can provide a welcome addition.

Agents

The use of agents is one of the most hotly debated marketing issues that international recruiters face. Some institutions view them as a logical requirement for successful overseas sales, drawing an analogy with the sale of cars or electrical goods. At the other end of the scale they can be viewed as crass, commercially driven, corrupt, exploitative, ill-informed and dangerous. They are seen as intrusive, and as out of place in the matching of students with courses as a marriage broker with clients who seek true love. Somewhere between the two extremes is the belief that they can be supportive, successful, student-centred and valuable partners, provided that sufficient time, effort, patience and resource is put into managing them.

Types of agent

To begin with, it should be recognized that the term 'agent' is loosely used by almost everyone. A dictionary definition of agent is 'One who or that which exerts power or produces an effect . . . one who acts for another'. In the context of education, this is not always the intended role.[10] The term 'agent' could be used to cover the activities of the British Council, or schools when they have materials in their careers library, or university and college international centres when they recommend postgraduate or exchange opportunities. In the main, however, these institutions are not motivated by commercial advantage at the point of sale. Of course, the British Council is representing UK institutions and a component of ECS performance analysis will be the numbers of students from that country registering in UK institutions. In the same way, schools wish to see all their students appropriately and happily placed and are able to represent the principal at the point of choice. These examples are not at the centre of the continuing debate. Nor indeed are the large consultancy groups who represent many of the institutions and undertake project work as well as recruitment. The controversy centres on the increasing numbers of travel agents, language organizations and individuals or groups receiving commission for the successful placement of students. The ease with which agencies can be set up, the lack of legislation or need for accreditation, the very small capital outlay required and the evidence of quick and substantial incomes all make this an alluring career choice for the individual – no matter how unsuitable he or she may be.

Rationale for use of agents

The reasons why any institution should consider working with an agent are obvious. Most institutions have limited budgets and limited staff time. An annual two-week visit to a country is at the luxury end of the contact scale, and if that country is the size of Brazil, China or Indonesia then two weeks can scarcely do more than develop contact in the capital city and perhaps one other centre of population. The need for information, advice and help with applications is constant. Chapter 5 considers the systems that should be in place at home if the marketing strategy is to work but even if these systems are of a high quality, supported with email and telephone responses, they are at one remove from the personal exchange and are normally carried on in a second language. If a good student is choosing between three good institutions and needs help with his or her application form or visa, or an immediate response to a question about accommodation, he or she is likely to feel favourably disposed to the institution which can provide the best immediate information and reassuring assistance. Being able to talk to a well-briefed compatriot in his or her own language in an office a couple of miles from home with immediate access to the principal for faxing applications and responses can be seen as a huge advantage by the uncertain student. This is also a 'free' service to the student. On the other hand, the student who is seeking information on courses as widely offered as, for example, the MBA would be well advised to look for objective and comprehensive advice from either the British Council or a business school accrediting organization or one of the few very large counselling institutions. Unless the student is clear about the range of courses available, to stumble into the office of an individual representing only one or two institutions is to be short changed. If the student has done the necessary research and knows which group of institutions to ask for information, then the presence of the agent can be extremely helpful. The agent wants a good income, the institution wants a growing number of well-qualified students registering from that country, who are able to pay the fees, and the student wants help, advice or hand-holding, so that all the procedures for admission to the appropriate course are painlessly completed. If it works, all three parties can be satisfied. If it falls apart then the living of the agent, the future of the student and the reputation of the institution are all at risk.

Selection of agents

Agents should be selected carefully but realistically.

- They should be persons of integrity with at least some interest in the UK and in education.
- They should be intelligent, quick to assimilate information, with good interpersonal skills and a manner appropriate to counselling.
- They must have sufficient command of English to communicate orally and in writing with the UK institution.
- They must have some understanding of the educational system in their own country.
- They should have office premises which are appropriate to the standing of the UK institution they represent and have demonstrable financial and business acumen.

With all these skills and personal qualities, anyone passing the agent appointment test might well earn ten times as much working outside education! In many countries, the ability to speak English to the required agency level would immediately open up higher salary opportunities. UK institutions should be aware that they are not looking for a post-doctoral education counselling specialist or someone who can draw up a five-year business plan suitable for Rolls Royce. They are looking for someone who has the confidence and enthusiasm to break out of the secretarial, routine sales or travel agency job, who has an ability to get on with people, sufficient English for social interaction and the talent for spotting opportunities. Sometimes a particular strength in counselling is accepted, even in the absence of any talent to develop the business further. In making the selection the UK institution is well advised to seek curriculum vitae and references and, if possible, to meet with the prospective agent and view the premises. Student expectations may differ between Tokyo and Nairobi but any office bearing the logo of an accredited UK institution should at least be clean, tidy and in a respectable area.

Contracts

A contract with the agent should set out as clearly and as briefly as possible the rights and responsibilities of each party to the agreement. If these need to be expressed in a paper longer than three or four pages, it is likely that there is a degree of distrust which may impede further developments. If it is too brief, there is nothing to rely on should difficulties occur. Although the contract is written as binding on both parties it is debatable whether in a court of law, and in a court whose judicial system is unfamiliar to one of the parties, the conditions can always be enforced. Having the contract drawn up with legal advice will ensure its legal integrity but could be costly and time-consuming. The intent of the document is to set guidelines for practice and responsibility, and to outline what will occur if the conditions are breached. Some considerations in the appointment of agents will include:

- whether it is contrary to any British Council advice to appoint a representative in that country;
- whether the quality of the agent in so far as can be judged will be prejudicial to the reputation of the UK institution;
- how and to whom the agent will work;
- whether exclusivity is required on either side.

The general opinion with regard to agents has changed and is continuing to change. At one time they were banned from some British Council exhibitions and in some countries, such as Singapore, advice was offered that their use was contrary to the good of UK plc. It is now becoming the view that agents should be harnessed rather than ignored, trained rather than isolated, and registered rather than rejected. In most countries it is difficult to believe that a few possibly understaffed British Council offices supplemented by regular visits by UK institutions for brief sorties to the major cities can do much more than raise the profile, support the students who come to them and provide a general strategic planning for the endeavour. The agent, if successful, is a permanent presence dedicated to one or more UK institutions who has time and interest to spend on marketing and counselling and follow-up. If unsatisfactory, on the other hand, he or she is a constant risk whose manifest neglect, misinformation and grasping cash practices will damage the UK principal.

Operating with agents

Much has been said of the requisite qualities of the agent. Once the appointment has been made, having examined curriculum vitaes, followed up references, met for a proper discussion and seen the premises from which the agent will operate, the institution must play its own part. This will include:

- comprehensive briefings;
- part-funded visits by the agent to the recruiting country;
- frequent and positive communication;
- an efficient system of dealing with enquirers and applications;
- realistic expectations and goals;
- appropriate supplies of selected literature.

Agents need training, reinforcement and support, and this maintenance service is essential to the success of the venture. Agents cannot know of the existence of additional courses outside the prospectus, changes in fees structure which are not explained, new facilities available at the institution, or of the success or happiness of their own nationals studying in that institution, unless the institution tells them. If they don't know, then prospective students can't know and a valuable marketing mechanism is under-exploited or lost altogether. It is often better not to provide information at all than to allow misinformation or out-of-date information to circulate. Equally important is the matter of agent accountability and this should be clearly understood on both sides from the beginning. The contract itself can be best made, perhaps, between the agent and his or her employer/line manager. This is often the International Officer or the section responsible for marketing and recruitment. It is questionable whether the head of the institution should be involved in these agreements.

It is not in the agent's own interest to send applications to individual departments. The agent cannot be expected to channel PhD applications to the appropriate department – indeed, that is often a difficult task even within the institution itself. A system has to be established for the receipt, acknowledgement and monitoring of applications, for prompt initial responses, for advice on likely acceptability and, eventually, for payment of commissions. Each institution will have a feel for what procedures will best suit its organizational structure and ethos. This needs to be clearly expressed to the agent and effectively and efficiently administered.

Contractual exclusivity is a difficult issue. The British Council will be operating in most countries where agents are located and, as indicated above, these activities are not mutually exclusive but can be complementary and supportive. The state of the market and the size of the country can dictate what is required. In a new market a degree of exclusivity may be helpful. Financial risks have to be taken by both sides. Agents setting up in Thailand in the 1980s or Myanmar in the 1990s may have to embark on so much fundamental groundbreaking work that they believe they alone should reap the rewards, when the time comes. On the other hand, agents in Turkey or Cyprus, at present, may believe that the systems are so well established that several outlets per institution can be sustained. This is very much a matter for negotiation and agreement between the agent and the principal and, with rolling contracts of two or three years, can be adjusted as the market changes. The size of the country in question is obviously a factor. The appointment of a sole agent in Brazil with exclusive rights to the whole country is risible. It would be a difficult enough task for one agent to cover the city of São Paulo with its 20 million inhabitants. On the other hand, someone located centrally in Singapore could make his or her presence felt throughout that small country. Exclusivity normally means that the main thrust of the institution's recruitment and marketing activities will be focused through the contracted agent. It does not mean, and should never mean, that the host institution cannot be approached by any individual or any local institution save through that agent.

Issues to be resolved

Agreements, therefore, have to be reached with absolute clarity on the following:

- Commission – how much, when and on what evidence?
- Charges to students – whether acceptable and, if so, how much and whether non-refundable?
- Advertising – at what cost and at whose instigation, and whose responsibility is it to write and vet the advertisement?
- Representational powers – where can the agents promote, to whom can they speak and with whom negotiate?

Commission

The level of commission has become generally accepted de facto. Ten per cent of the first year's paid-up tuition fees is now the norm. Language schools and those offering short courses or unusual delivery methods may set another figure. Some agents ask for higher commission on longer courses or for retainers in addition to the commission, or for target achievement bonuses. All of this rests on negotiation between the agent and the principal. It is worth pointing out, however, that an escalation of commission rates might well lead to a price war among the host institutions. This would serve only to increase the income of the agents, set institution against institution and create an unregulated jungle market in which students are directed to the highest paying institution rather than to the most appropriate. Of course, agents will be often provided with other and additional payments for long service, or special endeavours, or support with non-application tasks, but in calculating the level of commission the host institution should not forget how much they already commit to that country in marketing materials, attendance at exhibitions and student-centred activities such as scholarships and alumni hospitality. Successful agents can be extremely well remunerated on the ten per cent commission basis paid in, for example, US dollars in a lower cost economy. Occasionally, the remuneration rivals that of eminent senior professors in the home institution!

There should be a clear set of procedures for claiming and paying commission. The guidelines for this must, of course, fall within the institution's own financial regulations and should include:

- a full list of students advised to apply;
- a check on registration and fee payment by the host institutions;
- a check that the registered students have applied on the application form with the agent's stamp;
- the presentation of a detailed invoice by the agent.

In order to avoid time-consuming investigations and arid wrangling, it is helpful to agree at the beginning whether only applications carrying the agent's stamp can receive commission. The permutations outside the stamped form are myriad. Beware of embarking on possible time-consuming investigating of and acrimonious discussion in each case. Instead, a blanket fee for general assistance provided to all non-stamped applications can meet the need. Whatever the system, once verified, the commission should be paid promptly and at the agreed time. Within a few weeks of the beginning of the academic year or of the programme start, agreement should have been reached and the money should be on its way. Often the commission is only paid once a year and always in retrospect. The agent, therefore, has worked for twelve months without any tangible reward. Prompt payment helps to ensure loyalty for the following year and a continuing trust between agent and principal.

Student payment

The question of student payment to an agent is a more sensitive one. Counselling from the British Council is professional and objective and currently free so why do students seek out agents? Mainly, we believe, because they can provide a more personal, detailed and perhaps more accessible service. Agents will contact the institution daily, if necessary, and they will perform a handholding function at every stage. However, these agencies are often staffed by only one or two people and have no other source of income. They claim, therefore, that they must be able to dissuade time wasters and speculators in order to concentrate on serious applicants. They also claim that in some cultures, payment to a go-between is accepted and indeed expected. The host institution may choose to allow the agent to accept a small fee/deposit or may refuse to condone it. If a fee is to be charged, then the host institution must:

- have been informed in advance and have agreed to it;
- have agreed the size of the fee, which should be small;
- know and agree to the rules with regard to the return of the fee;
- know that applicants will be told in advance the agent's fee and also that direct application can be made to the institution without cost;
- monitor the situation for any evidence of student dissatisfaction with the system.

The amount of cash handled and the potential for damage to reputation are often in exact proportion.

Placing advertisements

The principal needs to remember that when an advertisement is published it speaks for the institution it represents. If it is misspelt, infelicitously phrased, appears in an inappropriate journal or is inaccurate and misleading, the student has a right to make certain assumptions about the quality of the institution. He or she will not believe it to be the fault of the agent. The contract should state, therefore, that any advertising materials have to be agreed in advance, in content, presentation and place of publication. If the advertisement is to be in the local language some arrangements might be made for checking the text, though it is less likely that spelling and grammatical mistakes will occur in the agent's first language.

There is no doubt that the preparation of an advertisement can reveal a clash of cultural perceptions. It is, for example, the British habit to be understated, and the requirement of the code of conduct to be accurate! It is unlikely, therefore, that a British institution would claim to be 'by far the best in the UK leaving all the others well behind'! Agents often have no such scruples. If they are selling it, it must be the best and they may see little need to worry about the intricacies of league tables or advertising standards. The principal has the final responsibility here. An agent who is working well with his UK principal could be asked to share the costs of advertising, or indeed less commonly bear the whole cost. His or her advice on suitable outlets for publicity is valuable since the agent will have considerable in-country experience. Again, however, it should not be accepted without thought. An advertisement in the wrong magazine may well bring the agent's name to the attention of a great many people, but very few of them will become students at the UK institution.

Many of the agent's applications may be rejected and the principal will have to decide what, if anything, the agent is expected to do with these. Should they be forwarded to the British Council for counselling and redirecting, or left with the agent to offer to other institutions in the UK or, indeed, to other countries, as the agent sees fit? It is not always to the principal's advantage to allow agents to offer rejected applicants to other institutions.

Representational powers
The institution has to decide, too, what is expected of the agent, bearing in mind the agent's perceived limitations. Is the agent to be merely the recipient of enquiry forms, probably generated at an exhibition or by advertisement, and which would lead to consultation and counselling? Agents with genuine counselling skills are valuable and this reactive role well executed may be as much as the institution can expect. On the other hand, the agent could:

- assist with business plans;
- feed through marketing information;
- learn how to give presentations in schools;
- make arrangements for in-country activities by the institution, such as alumni gatherings.

At the top of this ladder of desirable skills and trust comes the ability to give competent presentations to universities and sponsors, and the provision to the institution's management team of information and advice about all relevant issues relating to that country.

Any of these levels is acceptable if both parties understand the level at which they are working together. Agents exist to help the institution meet its agreed objectives in that geographical area. The most satisfactory methods of working with them are of collegiality and trust. Their work must complement the efforts of the institution and not prove prejudicial to them. In every case, there will be a need for initial training and education of the representative in the expectations and procedures of the institution and, equally importantly, of the institution in the customs and systems of the agent's country. This will be referred to again in Chapter 5.

In all of the above, the title 'agent' has referred to the commercial agent usually paid on commission and retained on a short-term contract. Some institutions, on the other hand, maintain members of staff permanently stationed around the world to represent them on a full-time basis in exactly the same way as would a visiting member of that institution. They are salaried and their performance is not judged solely, or indeed at all, by numbers of students recruited. They have a far wider and more demanding brief, often concerned with special projects and new developments. Sometimes appropriately staffed offices are established overseas from which these efforts can be directed. Each institution will decide whether the advantages of such arrangements justify the necessary cost and effort involved. The fact that more and more institutions are willing to allocate resources for this purpose demonstrates the growing importance accorded to international activities – and recognition of the ultimate value of a personal presence on the spot!

Conclusion

Agents are only one form of ambassador for an institution and in subsequent chapters alumni, current students, visiting colleagues, conference delegates, the embassies and national trade missions are all discussed. Whatever the size and competence of the group responsible for marketing and recruitment, it is almost always too small to carry the burden alone. Nor should it be expected to. Every member of the institutional community can enhance its reputation overseas with proper briefing and advice. Many in-country organizations can supplement the institutional effort. The main thrust can be directed by a small group, but it is far more likely to be successful if the talents and enthusiasm of all are harnessed to the international task.

Endnotes

1 International schools do not necessarily follow the same examination pattern. British schools customarily offer the A Level syllabus or, increasingly, the International Baccalaureate. American schools favour SATs with opportunities for APTs. American British academies may offer both. While the UK institutions have a clear policy with regard to A Level and IB, there is less knowledge of American qualifications.

2 It often proves impossible to equate the local transcript (exactly and consistently) with a UK degree. In some countries GPAs with a maximum of 5 are used; others with 4. Marks may be gained for areas of excellence unrelated to the academic subject, for example, community service or religious studies. Since UK institutions do not generally require standardized testing, such as the GRE in the United States, knowledge of precedent and of the quality of the individual department in the overseas institution is important. As a rule of thumb, the main institutions in the major cities are likely to be better staffed and to attract better students than those in the economically deprived regions of the same country.

3 The Malaysian secondary school leaving examination, Siji Tinggi Persekolaham Malaysia (STPM) is described by NARIC as satisfying the general entrance requirements of British higher education.

4 The British Council has convened a large number of such market surveys and this is one of the Council's activities with which subscribers regularly express a high level of satisfaction. A typical survey would be undertaken by an experienced practitioner in that area or by a consultant. Both would work with British Council staff on the ground. These are now supplemented by market plans. Information gathered and presented would include an executive summary, aims, objectives, economic and political background, market opportunities by sector, competitor activity and new opportunities. Several copies of the survey or plan are sent to each subscribing institution.

5 The Kenyan Certificate of Secondary Education admits students to a four-year undergraduate programme in the Kenyan universities. It is widely regarded by UK institutions as of a lower level than A Levels and thus requires a further period of studying before admission to the UK undergraduate system. Many of the school leaving qualifications, such as the KCSE, which examine a wider range of subjects (often 10) at this level cannot offer the depth in selected areas currently required as a prerequisite for undergraduate study in the UK. Throughout discussion of foundation courses it is to be noted that the Scottish universities can offer an integrated four-year undergraduate degree.

6 Collage of adverts for exhibitions culled from the most recent invitations and flyers:

> 'market leader in the field of international student recruitment marketing communications . . . a unique opportunity to recruit students from . . . leading source of international students through a cost and time-efficient circuit covering seven major population centres . . .'

'the most important and effective guide to study abroad for students from . . .'

'building on the phenomenal success of last year's event . . .'

'no other education site has ever had this much promotion'

'the prime source of information about overseas study . . .'

'Can you accept some additional qualified fully funded students from Asia for the coming semesters?'

7 In the calendar year 1998 the British Council (ECS) is coordinating a schedule of 47 exhibitions and promotional events, by subject, by sector and by region. These cover both established markets and new venues. In many countries they include events in a number of cities. Some countries attract several types of mission in a year, e.g. Malaysia has a generic exhibition in four cities, a clearing mission and a postgraduate exhibition.

8 The British Council Code of Practice published in 1989, and subsequently revised, listed among the areas for consideration:

- the principles of and policy for recruitment,
- academic policy issues;
- marketing;
- the quality of information provided;
- the manner in which students were admitted;
- the level of support services offered.

Further codes relating to quality and to overseas links have also been produced more recently. In addition, the Overseas Student Trust and UKCOSA were in the forefront of organizations advocating 'responsible recruitment'.

9 British Council Offices overseas make available on request copies of the most recent Research Assessment Exercise and the Teaching Quality Assessment. The full text with the gradings explains the procedures and their timing, criteria and significance. Other ratings, such as those of the *Times* and the *Financial Times*, are frequently widely read within the country and no institution should market abroad without being aware of its place (and its commentary on its place!) in these rankings. The FT league table published in April 1998 states,

> The FT 100 is a snapshot of university performance across 16 categories, from entry requirements to library expenditure . . . the figures are drawn from published statistics . . . The FT 100 table measures performance on a relative – rather than an absolute – basis. It includes sub-tables on top provincial universities and top former polytechnics.

10 Bruce Cherry Associates prepared some interesting definitions in this area to which this paragraph alludes.

4

REPEAT ORDERS: LOOKING AFTER STUDENTS

Introduction

Rolls Royce would not sell cars without provision for continuing after-sales care. Educationalists would not encourage young people to travel across the world to live and study without providing a generous level of supportive care. Commercial good sense and responsible humanity come together in the preparation of the proper package for our international students. Secure and happy students are more likely to be academically successful, to enjoy good memories of their time overseas and so to become satisfied customers. Satisfied customers, their families, friends and sponsors are in a position to generate repeat sales. Happy students who are well integrated create fewer problems for themselves and their institutions and so the institutions are better disposed to accept an increasing number of international students. Above and beyond all this, the host institutions are staffed by colleagues who are interested in people and dedicated to education. Any dereliction of duty to students and lack of care for, or understanding of, the international student is at odds with all of these mission statements and professional standards. The need to provide a proper level of care is, therefore, self-evident. The methods by which it is provided have been learned over a long period and no one institution can claim to do it all, or to know it all. Needs vary, customs change and attitudes alter. An institution can only intend to act properly, take advice from organizations who are specialists in this area,[1] resource the implementation of the commitment to care and keep it continually under review.

The course begins ■

Before arrival

Keeping in touch

Even if the student has already visited the exhibition stand, the British Council or the commercial agent, he or she may well need further assurances and detailed information before making the application, accepting the offer and finally arriving at the institution for registration. The requests for information may be entirely legitimate or they may simply be a cry for reassurance – an expression of anxiety at the idea of trusting a life plan to an institution 8000 miles away with whom face-to-face contact has only briefly, if ever, been made. For the International Office or the External Affairs section receiving perhaps 700 queries a month, or for the admissions tutors busy with the current demands of the students, the volume of enquiries and follow-up questions by mail, fax, telephone and now email often seems overwhelming. The responses to these queries, however, are the small scraps of evidence on which the international student builds his or her initial impression of the institution. If a reply never comes, if it is curt or fails to answer the questions or is quite blatantly mass produced, then the impression gained can be one of a factory rather than a community. Some of the information, too, is vital for its own sake. Details about housing, schools for children, National Health provision, visa requirements, length of time required in pre-sessional language training, preliminary reading or necessary clothing are essential in the run-up to departure.

Reassurance for applicants

Much time and duplication of effort can be saved if a carefully prepared booklet or set of booklets is available and mailed to applicants as appropriate. The content should include such practical details as how to travel from airports to the institution. Timetables, prices and general points of clarification are important here. However comprehensive the literature, it does not dispense with the need to respond quickly, helpfully, individually and warmly to every student query. Some communications too will be generated by the host institution and, like so many other activities in this chapter, should be a fortunate blend of student care and marketing. One specific example of UK-generated mail relates to applicants. The UCAS system does not necessitate written contact between the institution and the applicant. The data is electronically compiled and passed on, and indeed there was believed under the rules to be a discouragement of interaction between applicant and admissions tutor. This is not the case; on the contrary, it is an excellent practice for the formal offer to be followed by a letter from the tutor, the Faculty Office or the International Office. The applicant is reassured that there are real people at the end of the computer line and the impression conveyed in the period between the institution making an offer and the student electing to go 'firm', 'insurance', or 'reject' may well affect this important decision. Institutions should realize that they are not at this point simply trying to influence student choice to themselves in preference to the other five institutions on the UCAS form but, more importantly, they are persuading the student that the UK, rather than Australia or the USA, will best meet his or her expectations or requirements. The UCAS system, while having considerable strengths, is not user friendly or transparent to the international student. Discussions are now taking place which may lead to changes within the system but in the meanwhile any action that could ease the obfuscation and bureaucracy is welcome. It should be remembered that the competitor systems are often accessible through a single application form sent to the institution of choice.

Additional details

In the UK, application procedures for FE and postgraduate courses are more straightforward than those for undergraduate study. Packs of information carefully prepared to be culturally specific can be sent out during the pre-registration period. Parents and students will be pleasurably surprised to receive a booklet detailing Islamic facilities, if they are likely to require them, or listing the activities of the appropriate national society at the university. Such packaging requires a degree of knowledge and competence in the sending office. It would not be helpful, for instance, to send details of halal outlets to every student from a country such as Turkey or Malaysia or information on the Greek Society to students from North Cyprus. Admission tutors have often found it helpful to provide handouts for students from the larger sending countries which detail the numbers of students from these countries in the institution and academic links that exist. Names and addresses of agents can be sent and students encouraged to contact them for additional useful information. This depends upon the quality and reliability of the agent as discussed in the preceding chapter. The proactive approach can be taken with letters and packages of information to all students who have received an offer and, again, when they have accepted that offer. Part-year exchange and study abroad students can be sent a 'welcome to the institution' letter two or three weeks before departure to the UK. This is especially important for students who begin their study at times other than the start of the academic year.

Logistics

It is debatable whether it is better for all communications to come from one office (a one-stop shop) or to arrive from a number of sources. The advantage of the former method is that the information will be consistent and the sender will become a recognized point of contact for the student. The disadvantage is that the sheer volume of correspondence imposes a tremendous burden on a single office. The advantage of the latter dispersed scheme is that the student gains an impression of a diverse institution with a team of colleagues – in the Faculty, in Accommodation, in the Students' Union, in the International Office – all extending help and information. The disadvantage is that this method can create an impression of uncoordinated chaos with pieces of information of various sizes, shapes and quality arriving at random intervals and often duplicating or even contradicting one another. Any scheme should aim for the efficiency of centralization with the individual warmth which should mark the responses from a variety of offices.

In dealing with the pre-arrival needs of individual students, the wishes of sponsors should not be forgotten. Funding agencies, intermediaries and other such organizations need to gather information, either to inform their own budgetary decisions or to help in advising the student. Again, leaflets on tuition fees, accommodation arrangements, term dates and insurance requirements can be very helpful both in reducing the load on the host institution and providing immediate information to the enquirer.

Both the British Council (often working with alumni groups) and more and more commercial agents will now organize in-country pre-departure briefings. The host institution should provide as much help for these as possible, both by sending literature and inviting to the event, and encouraging to contribute, existing students who are here for the holiday, and new graduates returning home. These events not only provide an opportunity for the disseminating of factual information about the UK but also help the travellers to make friends, plan economic travel arrangements and generally gain confidence from the peer group. Everything positive that was said about alumni at exhibitions in Chapter 3 can be repeated here. As satisfied customers, they and current students make invaluable ambassadors.

Pre-arrival care must include full and honest details about accommodation. Indeed honesty is one of the prime requirements of any information provided by the institution. The opposite invariably comes home to roost in the end! If family housing is difficult to obtain and in limited supply, it is essential to say so. Better by far to lose before registration a prospective student who is put off by the clearly announced limit to family accommodation, than later to have an angry student with family who has discovered that the marketed 'plentiful accommodation' is for single occupancy only. Accommodation is one of the key concerns of all international students and any guarantees should be clearly spelt out at every opportunity before arrival.

By the end of August, the vast majority of international students intending to study in the UK should have received their offers, gained their pre-arrival qualifications, made their decisions and begun to prepare for travel to begin the new academic year. Some sponsors, however, make late decisions on the provision of funding and, as the economic situation in some areas worsens, this may become more frequent. In addition, some students for undergraduate courses continue to ignore UCAS, miss UCAS deadlines or go directly into the clearing system. To respond to both these circumstances and to increase the UK market share, many UK institutions now attend in August late recruitment/clearing missions run by the British Council and others in Malaysia, Hong Kong, Cyprus and Turkey. Candidates entering as a result of those measures need accurate information most urgently and those responsible for providing it must be aware that the regular airmail procedures cannot be relied on. Whenever possible, faxes, emails and even telephone calls should be used to put the students' minds at rest. Good marketing practice, humane concerns and effective procedures in this area have all now found additional endorsement in the Dearing Committee Report (NCIHE 1997).

On arrival

It is sometimes easy to forget the acute and often painful meld of culture shock, jetlag and home sickness that can afflict students on their arrival at the port or airport. For some students it will be their first visit to the overseas destination, others will only have been here with their parents or bolstered by the organization of a group visit. Many will be no more than 18 years old, some as young as 17. Many will travel alone. For some few it will be their first experience of flying and, for most, of long-haul flight and time zone change. No matter how well prepared the student has been in terms of the pre-arrival literature and counselling, nothing is quite the same as arrival in the new country. As a people, we may seem to ourselves entirely rational and straightforward: to a young person from the other side of the world, however, we may at first appear strange and distant to a degree which would surprise us.

There is much discussion of the cultures that will experience the most acute form of culture shock on arrival in the UK. It is to be expected that students from the USA or from other first language English-speaking countries will feel most at home. Perhaps students from Europe who are only travelling within the continent will feel a certain assurance. Those arriving from Commonwealth countries may feel an affinity with the UK. Nevertheless, the simple fact seems to be that *all* students need and value support offered instantly on arrival.

Transport on arrival

The support offered should be both practical and moral. Anyone who has witnessed the amount of luggage which a single student can transport and is familiar with the complex business of getting from airport to institution will appreciate the need for dedicated transport. The logistics of this for a large institution with a single collection day are considerable but manageable. Coaches can be laid on to meet every flight (many flights from the East tend to arrive between 5.30 and 8.00 a.m. UK time) and these coaches should be accompanied by lorry luggage carriers. It is difficult and dangerous to pack students and luggage on the same vehicle. Coaches can be escorted by staff or students who see the activity as part of the welcome package. Identifying sweatshirts or T-shirts give the whole thing a touch of fun and glamour. The success of the collection operation depends on the quality of the information system set up for the welcome package. If the right number of coach seats is to be provided then a proper database needs to be set up with input during the preceding month. The provision of institutional staff in the airport can help any students who have difficulties with papers at immigration. It is sometimes possible to provide assistance to students being questioned 'airside'. The British Council offers a meet and greet scheme which welcomes student arrivals and points them in the right direction for onward transport. It is easier if the institution's coaches depart at regular intervals rather than in convoy, but sometimes difficult to persuade the drivers of this! Single coaches, disembarking students and luggage at regular intervals throughout the day ensure a much less frenetic atmosphere than groups of five or six coaches disgorging simultaneously at one registration point. Smaller institutions, or those faced with widely dispersed arrival points on several different dates, may not feel able to collect their students in dedicated coaches. There are usually ways around this, however, and the importance of proper support at the point of arrival should not be underestimated – even if the cost in terms of time and resources is high. In many cases institutions could work together with two or three of them taking it in turns to provide coaches for a regional grouping.

Clear and precise travel details should be sent out in good time to all new international students. This should be done whether or not a coach is available, as not all students, no matter how careful the planning, will arrive on the right day. Some countries, for instance, repeatedly state that they cannot guarantee which airline a student will be travelling on until close to the departure date. Such pre-arrival literature should explain the use of words like 'tube', and make clear the amount of money required for the journey and the time that it will take. Detailed extracts from rail and coach timetables will be helpful. It is difficult and dispiriting for a student alone, and encumbered with luggage, to wander around an unfamiliar station seeking the information in a second language after a 12-hour flight. Pre-arrival information will have suggested the amount of money in local currency that the student should be carrying on arrival, assuming that this will be enough to last for at least a couple of days while bank arrangements are being set up. As mentioned earlier, the British Council can be available to meet students and, even if the institution cannot organize a coach to collect its students, it can arrange for a member of staff to be available at the airport. Students arriving late on the day prior to the coach pick-up could be advised to stay near the airport for the night and to pick up the coach in the morning. If an institution finds it difficult to afford a free coach service, it might consider setting a small charge per traveller – but beware the complications of collecting such a sum, and the dilemma posed by a student who does not have the cash available!

Undoubtedly, the best solution for the majority of students is the provision of free transport that collects them at a convenient time, looks after their luggage and carries an easily identified representative of the institution to handle small anxieties and practical problems. All of this assumes a standard start date (generally at the beginning of the academic year) and students travelling without family. More and more postgraduates are bringing spouses and children with them to the UK, although in many cases the student will arrive first and make arrangements for the family to follow at a later date. Many more students, too, are joining the host institutions for part-year studies – either for a term or a semester. European and US students currently form the bulk of this group but this pattern of attendance is likely to increase. Those students arriving in January, February or April should not be ignored. It is to be expected, too, that the European students may arrive at the smaller local airports or at seaports or the Channel Tunnel terminal. They often have the advantage of travelling together under the aegis of an exchange or study abroad arrangement. Research students can begin at any time of the year, and a single student arriving on a dark, wet January afternoon will need special care.

The welcome package

No matter by what means students make their way to the institution, arrival should be built into a welcome and orientation package. This is not solely for the benefit of the student. Institutions which deliver well-constructed welcome packages report that they experience less difficulty with student integration in the following weeks and spend far less time responding to individual queries and anxieties. The impression of warmth and efficiency made on the student, and the caring introduction to overseas academic life which is offered, are of paramount importance. A welcome programme is designed to reflect the ethos of the institution and there can be no single pattern suitable for all. Some guidelines, however, can be offered.

- As far as possible, this programme should be provided to *all* new international students, regardless of fee status. The feeling of vulnerability and isolation may be the same for an exchange as for a PhD student, for a Greek as for a Cypriot. Financial constraints are a fact of life, but at this point of arrival in a new country, need rather than resourcing should direct provision. Again, experience shows that well-acculturated students adjust more easily and save time and anxiety later on in the year.
- As far as possible, the programme should be offered without charge for all items that can be reasonably included. Accommodation may be covered but not necessarily all meals. Entrance fees to cinemas or bowling alleys may not be included, but coach trips to local sites could well be. All talks and campus-based activities should be offered without charge. This allows and encourages maximum numbers to attend and so to benefit.
- Staff and registered students (both home and overseas) should work together. Some institutions place the organization and resourcing of the welcome package with the Students' Union or the international student league; others through some office in the administration. The combination of staff and students working together allows opportunity for mutually valuable exchange of ideas and

experiences and brings to the final package enthusiasm, energy, system and authority. It becomes a truly institutional offering.

- The programme should allow time for recovery, social interaction, task completion, knowledge gain, personal support and fun. Ice-breaking sessions can be a good idea on the arrival night but a late breakfast and a free morning is also useful on the second day. However resilient and excited an 18-year-old may be, travel and change can be stressful and exhausting, and built-in opportunities for catching up with sleep are important. There will be a number of tasks which have to be completed and, although tedious, they are vital. Registration with the police and the GP is important (to meet specific immigration requirements) and an arrangement with the bank is essential. If accommodation has not been secured, then interviews with the Accommodation Office and the search for suitable housing is of key importance and ranks highest among student priorities. The programme provides an opportunity to acquire information on the administrative systems within the institution – where a registration will take place, what the credit rating system will be, when the students can select their modules, how they join the Union and access sports facilities. Academic staff, tutors and supervisors may explain the teaching styles and methods of assessment. Either individually or in small groups, students can be introduced to the support and welfare services, chaplains can mix at meal times, counsellors and advisers can make themselves available over coffee and give clear information on the health service, recreational facilities, faculty support and language remediation. At the same time, home and international students can help with all the student meetings and organize the social activities. The provision of early opportunities to meet fellow students, to develop contacts and begin friendships is a vital ingredient of the package. The amount of unstructured time should be sufficient to allow privacy and rest but not enough to allow isolation or anxiety.
- The programme should have a culmination and a climax. There should be a sense of having successfully come through this initial phase and of being prepared and confident to embark on the next. This can be achieved by a formal meal at the end of the period, when the highest ranking officer available in the institution and a broad range of colleagues can be invited. The opportunity to wear national dress, to dine formally, to observe the importance that the institution accords to its international links all heighten a sense of achievement and confidence. The first hurdle is over.
- The programme should not be so long that it becomes repetitive or slackens in pace, nor should it clash with the welcome being

offered by the institution to new home students. It is important
that the international students emerge from the 'incubator' of the
international welcome programme eager to see themselves next
as new students in the wider context and a part of the whole
community. The international and home welcome events should
complement one another as preparation for a common student
experience.

- All the events should be planned with sensitivity to intercultural
diversity. There must be an awareness of what is offensive or
embarrassing for the various cultures taking part without, however, losing the opportunity to express and teach about what is
considered essential to an understanding of the overseas way of
life. It must be recognized that social activities centred around
alcohol will make attendance impossible for some students and
unacceptable to others. The bar is, however, an important part of
social life and functions as a social centre in many university
residences. Bars now sell coffee and soft drinks and, in many
cases, food as well and thus the bar can cease to become out
of bounds for almost all of the constituency. Mixed swimming
sessions might be difficult if it is the one sporting activity. Ten-
pin bowling would be less so. A barn dance may be more acceptable than a disco. Menus with plenty of vegetarian food, fish and
poultry circumvent to some degree the need for halal or hillel.
These are considerations for the first few days of life abroad and
are intended to be supportive and reassuring. No one is suggesting
that the banning of pork or beef from any institutional food outlet would be helpful as a permanent measure. Students do find
their own ways of surviving happily and keeping their own beliefs
intact while enjoying a lifestyle in the new country. They do,
however, need help at the beginning. It may be worthwhile, too,
to include a talk, sensitively compiled and delivered, on what we
may call 'the way of life'. Most problems occur when mores are
misunderstood or their importance misinterpreted. An institution
confident in its own concern and care for international students
can talk to newcomers with insight, frankness and kindness about
bathroom and toilet habits and what is likely to give rise to friction and offence. It is just as important, but easier, to discuss, for
example, the British view on the use of 'please' and 'thank you'
(they like frequent repetition of these words); the attitude to women
in authority (it is the person, not the gender that matters); the
approach to manual or catering staff (they are employees, not
servants); the expectation on receiving a social invitation (reply
and then stick to it); and the custom with regard to punctuality
(lectures, appointments and meals begin on time unless otherwise

stated). Some hints on the British attitude to religion, politics, sport and the weather also help social intercourse! The most effective of these talks are often those where awareness of the humorous, the ridiculous and the idiosyncratic in one's own culture ameliorates any appearance of adverse comparison to another's.

- These programmes are expensive in terms of planning, implementation, manpower and money and their success is dependent on the value afforded to them by the participants. Evaluation in as formal a manner as possible is therefore important, both to ensure that the institution can feel justified in continuing to support them, and even to expand them, and to capture any constructive criticism or dissatisfaction and thus to build in new ideas and proposals. Sensibly succinct but itemized evaluation forms should be provided, and their completion and return assured. Scrutiny of the contents and scores is, of course, required once the forms are returned. Acculturation packages cannot be static in content – their composition must be constantly reviewed in order to respond to changes in host habits and values and to the mix of the nationalities and creeds attending.

On course

After collection, arrival and welcome, the student should be in all senses 'on course' for his or her degree. If the welcome package looks after many of the acute issues, then the on-course provision should offer a permanent infrastructure to manage continuing concerns. It should allow difficulties to be identified before they grow out of proportion and offer a network of care that allows students to select the most appropriate or acceptable point of contact. Welfare, care and support exist in each institution for every student and the holistic approach to UK further and higher education is one of its identifying and successful characteristics. International students, however, face additional and specific challenges, and the meeting of their needs requires careful planning and thoughtful and often expensive execution.

Accommodation

Needs and definitions

All students regard the provision of residential accommodation as a high priority. This does not necessarily mean that the institution needs to own all the accommodation that is required but that it should manage, facilitate, inform and assist. Students living in the country have an opportunity to look at properties before they register on their programme. They often have a knowledge of the geographical area and have an understanding of the system. They often, too, have family support and a network of friends who can assist. The UK is not a large country and even students travelling from Aberdeen to an institution in Exeter can be expected to have some background knowledge of that region, the legal system relating to tenancy and licence, some understanding of the British halls of residence, some concept of central heating and urban garden maintenance. Such a basic level of knowledge cannot be expected of all international students, although a proportion of them may well be familiar with all these and many other factors.

In the main, international students will arrive in the institution for the first time on the day that the welcome programme begins; many still arrive on the first day of teaching. Most institutions which are able to do so will guarantee accommodation to new undergraduate students. The students may be asked in advance if they wish to accept institutional accommodation and which type of accommodation they would prefer. So many of the descriptions and phrases that indigenous students take for granted may be unfamiliar to new international students, reading the papers in a second language and with no family member close by who has experienced the same system. When describing the type of accommodation, the literature should be clear and descriptive, ensuring that students understand:

- university-owned halls of residence (known sometimes as dormitories);
- university-owned flats or houses (sometimes known as student villages/ residences);
- private sector accommodation (sometimes identified as digs, bedsits, housing association, hostels, shared flats and houses);
- university-owned or private sector married accommodation.

The student will need to know:

- whether any or all are self-catering;
- what facilities are provided;
- what they are expected to bring with them;
- whether the rooms are single occupancy;
- what the bathroom facilities include and whether they are shared;
- whether the accommodation is single-sex or mixed;
- whether the accommodation is on-campus or at some distance.

They will also wish to know the cost, both of the accommodation on offer and of the extra requirements. If the price of self-catering flats is indicated, then the student may well wish to know the average cost of a weekly shopping basket.

Much of this information is provided before arrival and the student assimilates it as he or she prepares for departure. For many undergraduates other students from their school may have attended the same institution: information (and indeed equipment) is often passed from year to year. National student associations can also be excellent at providing student-centred information and this can form an important part of the welcome programme. Institutions which have retained a combination of single- and mixed-sex residences in the face of the 1970s rush to mix them all will find a demand for this single-sex option from Muslim students and parents. Those who have moved to more generous en-suite building or refurbishment will find this option popular with both home and international students. While the HE institutions have long believed in the advantage of a residential community and have taken the initiative in building and maintaining a variety of residence options, a decline in financial support for home students, a likely increase in part-time and mature student numbers and a growing belief in some sectors in the advantages of attending the local institution may well mean that the existing stock will be under-subscribed. This could be seen as advantageous to international students who could gain a greater share of the existing provision, with possible guarantees of accommodation for the whole of the undergraduate period. It could prove disadvantageous, however, if residences became international 'ghettos' and consequently students lost the opportunity to live and socialize together, either in university-owned accommodation or subsequently in shared flats and houses.

Colleges of FE and sixth-form colleges are likely to be less generously provided with institutional accommodation. The specific need to select, maintain and monitor landlady accommodation or dedicated housing is therefore critical. When this is done well, however, it can provide one of the most important factors in the student's overseas experience. A caring and welcoming host family can provide a level of friendship and support which is remembered and valued by both host and student for a lifetime. Heads of State across the world have spoken fondly of the British landlady.

Postgraduates and families

Postgraduates, and especially those with accompanying families, face the keenest of the accommodation difficulties. This is partly a result of their age and seniority. 18-year-olds leaving home for the first time generally gain a great deal from communal living. They have time to take advantage of the expanded horizons and rich experiences that a full social and recreational life can bring. Postgraduates, on the other hand, are often following one-year masters programmes with considerable work pressures and have responsibilities to employers or families (either back at home or with them overseas). They often hold senior rank in their own country and as a result can be used to a lifestyle far different from that offered in university postgraduate accommodation. They may not, however, possess the necessary resources to replicate that lifestyle in the UK. They can, therefore, become a group more difficult to integrate into an existing accommodation system. Many will appreciate university and postgraduate accommodation, particularly if this is a little removed from undergraduate housing. They may wish to arrive singly and live in institutional accommodation for a couple of months before seeking family accommodation. All of this creates difficulties for an accommodation office but is quite understandable from the student's point of view.

Family accommodation is often difficult to obtain and to manage. Older building stock can be costly for the institution to maintain and expensive for the student family to heat and furnish. There can be problems with neighbours, ranging from irritation to threats of, and actual, physical abuse. Often, an institution finds that one way of avoiding some of these problems is to manage its own purpose-built family accommodation, providing a well-run, safe and pleasant environment that can only enrich a student family experience.

Allocation and integration

If an institution can provide accommodation, it should also consider how it is to be allocated. There has been an argument advanced that an International House could be created where international students would be offered accommodation, and which could become a focus for international activity and social interaction. Examples of good practice in this regard can be found in London. On the other hand, international students are part of the student community and, for all the reasons rehearsed in other sections of this book, benefit accrues to all students from properly facilitated integration.

Integration, however, does not imply separation from compatriots. Support, especially in the first year of residence, can be provided by placing two or three students from the same country or region together. In some cases, too, the ablutions or the cooking regime of one particular religion or nationality may make it prudent to accommodate them together for the harmonious use of shared bathrooms and kitchens.

With this portfolio of demands and variables, pity the Accommodation Officer juggling with guarantees, students arriving alone and then to be joined by their families, single-sex requirements, small nationality groupings, the desire for multinational integration, illiberal or bigoted neighbours, separate lifestyles of undergraduates and postgraduates and the overriding need for the whole package to pay its way. As with most other issues relating to international students, when dealing with accommodation it is vital for the institution to be open to learning about needs and preferences, to be honest and comprehensive in the details sent in advance to students and to be supportive and consistent in the care offered to them.

Language support

All host institutions will need to be satisfied of a minimum level of language competence before a non-first language speaker commences on an academic programme. Indeed, it could be said that most institutions require evidence of linguistic competence from all students but that more particular attention is paid to the verification of this in the case of international students.

Gaining language proficiency

As has been noted in so many previous occasions in this chapter, what is best for the student is best for the institution. The level of language required for academic success has been discussed in earlier chapters but the social necessity of language is equally important. Breaking the barrier of reserve which is supposed to surround the British will be difficult enough, but breaking it in a meaningful manner with a poor command of English is impossible. If the student is to stand a chance of integration and of enjoying an experience of value beyond the educational qualification, then that student must speak the English language sufficiently well to allow conversation at a deeper than superficial level. It was believed when recruitment began that students could and would gain the necessary linguistic qualification for entry in their own country. This was, and continues to be, the cheapest method of acquiring the second language. It is not, however, the most effective, and more and more institutions have set up departments or centres which offer pre-sessional (that is prior to the date of registering for the academic qualification) courses. A language school too, *per se*, offers a focus for such learning. The advantage of improving English language

skills in the host country is that of total immersion. The students
live in the country and have the formal language lessons reinforced
whenever they ride on public transport, go shopping, turn on the
television or meet a neighbour. Language and culture become a
single issue which is not only learned but lived.

This level of language can be achieved in a specialist language
school as well as in the appropriate department of the academic
institution. The advantage of the latter, however, for the students
wishing to gain British academic qualifications is that they can become, as soon as they begin the language programme, members of
the community which is to be their ultimate study destination.
Generally, these pre-sessional language students have all the rights
and privileges of 'regular' students, which often include accommodation. English language classes include study skill and acculturation
topics, and the language class is enriched by appropriate reference
to the academic subject of study. Students can use these one to six
months not only to acquire the language level required but also to
make friends, meet the academic department to be the final destination, gain a quasi-specialist vocabulary and become familiar with
the institution, including the library. It is often acceptable to the
institution for these students not to be required to retake TOEFL
(Test of English as a Foreign Language) or IELTS (International
English Language Testing Service) at the end of the pre-sessional
programme, but to progress to the desired academic department by
virtue of the assignments and assessments offered through the language centre. Thus, while standards are maintained the students are
not subjected, unless they specifically require it, to the additional
stress of a further formal unseen test. Institutions which offer such
pre-sessional English do so as part of the total institutional provision, and so the quality of the English language course should equate
to the quality norms of other departments. 'Equate to' does not mean
'be the same as', and these departments have their own accreditation quality standards and class size appropriate to their objectives.
It is not always necessary for them to be staffed with colleagues
included in the Research Assessment Exercise, or with a majority of
tenured staff. It is necessary that the institution whose name they
carry is as content with their performance as with that of any other
department, however that is measured.

Locating the language centre

The location (geographic and organizational) of the department is
again a matter for discussion, and the latter is often a direct result of
the history or serendipity of its origin. Most people will agree that a

central, easily accessible, user friendly geographical location is important, with the possibility of out-posting or regular surgeries for students from far-flung parts of the institution. The location of that department or centre within the organization is more difficult to recommend. Should it be a part of an academic department such as English or Linguistics, or part of a modern language centre, or seen as a support service with the same status as the library and the computing centre? The advantages and disadvantages of each can be identified, but the overriding concern is that it should be of high quality and recognize which parts, if any, of its enterprise are income-generating and cost-recovering. Serving, on many occasions, as a bridge between the academic department and the student, it must act with due regard for standards and with integrity in assessing them. If the departments are to rely on the language teaching facility, that facility must reflect the quality of the institution and must not sacrifice standards for the sake of commercial success.

The other aims of the centre include student care and marketing. Students who come to the host country with less than functional English are even more vulnerable than their more linguistically competent colleagues. Welfare and pastoral care are offered alongside language acquisition and the staff of the language department provide key support. In a small unit where students can come to know one another and the staff, where limited class size is necessary for teaching, where all the students are new to the country and where teaching skills as opposed to research strengths are rated highly, a sympathetic atmosphere can be created in which students feel secure to learn, to question and to develop. The ease of progression from language student to a member of an academic department is one of the advantages of these institutional programmes. Quite often, too, the welcome afforded by the English centre to students arriving in January, April or July is their first experience of study in that country. The English centre, therefore, becomes the 'face' of the institution and all the more important for the first impression it makes. Its marketing materials, support provision, facilities and teaching quality make a considerable impact on the new student which only gradually fades as the academic course progresses.

An activity which began in the HE and FE sectors as language preparation for academic study has, as a result of the increasing entrepreneurship of the institutions, extended its scope. Such centres now often offer language courses of a stand-alone nature either of many months' duration or one month in the summer, specifically tailored programmes to meet professional needs and group courses on request. Many have the energy and ability to bid for and gain projects, either alone or with academic departments. Some offer 'English plus' courses leading to qualifications or credits in, for example, British studies or English and business. They offer competition to the language schools and have become a further income-generating activity of the entrepreneurial institution.

Ongoing support

Ensuring that students reach the right level of language on entry to the academic programme is, however, meeting only part of the student and institutional need. Many of the students who have gained the minimum requirement will lack confidence in the use of language, and will look for additional competence and reassurance. Academic departments, too, will want to believe that the students who have joined them will have the maximum linguistic support available to them. If the institution has, as part of its plan, an increasing proportion of international students, it will only help to convince departments of the benefits of accepting them if continuing support of all kinds is available to them. The language department or centre should, therefore, offer in-sessional language support which provides not only language enhancement but also classes on seminar presentation, examination techniques and thesis writing. Sometimes even first reading of the submitted work to check for linguistic deficiencies is offered. The language centre can provide a venue for social interaction, a feeling of 'coming home', where all kinds of issues can be aired outside what may be considered the assessment-driven atmosphere of the academic department.

Students who hold only the minimum language requirement on entry may not be able to cope with the realities of language use – the presence of dialect, the less than perfect articulation, the speed of the lecture, the confusion of speech in the babble of club or pub. The in-sessional support provided should enable students to become sufficiently confident and fluent to meet academic requirements, to enjoy conversation with first language speakers and to relieve their academic tutors of anxieties about their contribution to debate and ability to submit written work. Such support should also include information on the cultural diversity in approaches to learning and assessment. This is clearly central to any programme of study skills and can be offered by a central unit or by the department and staff concerned. Students should be informed of the pedagogic fundamentals of overseas education which value the analytical and questioning approach to knowledge rather than the received or rote learning style. Some students from some cultures will bring an uncritical reverence for the written word or the views of the teacher which might impede intellectual progress. An early indication of this view is often seen in the manner in which students quote from acknowledged source material. In some education systems it seems that the ability to reproduce an argument, often without formal attribution, is meritorious. In the UK and many other systems submitted work which incorporates substantial unacknowledged quotation from printed sources might be viewed as plagiarized. Students need careful counselling on this different approach.

The institution must recognize the additional role that such a centre is fulfilling by taking account of the in-sessional teaching load. The student should expect that the in-sessional support is provided without extra charge, but this facility is labour-intensive and consequently expensive to provide. A real commitment to student satisfaction and success could include the proper resourcing of the English language centre, to take account of its provision of this valuable but 'free' service. The role of English teaching to students' spouses is covered later in the chapter.

Healthcare

Entitlement

Britain is known in many areas of the world as a country with an enviable level of healthcare freely available to all its citizens. One of its advantages as a destination for overseas study is the National Health Service. The provisions of the NHS for international students are, however, more complex than may at first appear and are likely to become even more so.

Currently, Britain does not require compulsory medicals for students, either in their own country or at the point of entry. Exceptions to this are, in general, the same as are made for home students and these are normally related to students working in the areas of health or the care of children. Chest x-rays, freedom from certain conditions and hepatitis checks are required for teachers or those in the health professions. Students who cannot satisfy these requirements may not register for the courses. Once they are registered, however, the NHS will be responsible for the treatment of *all* international students and their immediate families resident in this country on courses of six months or longer. The institution, therefore, should be prepared to make the situation clear to intending students, to assist in making treatment accessible and to stand ready to protect both affected students and the wider community. The 'immediate family' is interpreted as spouses and children 16 years and under or children in full-time education. This position, like much else relating to health issues, is likely to be reviewed by the government.

While an adequate level of care is necessary for all students there are obvious special needs for international students where family support is unavailable, where cultural expectations may be different and where endemic illnesses and susceptibility to new infections may create additional vulnerability. Clear information should be provided for all students, again before arrival if possible, outlining what they can expect from the NHS. It should indicate for students staying less than six months that health insurance is absolutely essential. The system will always respond to emergencies and, unlike in some other countries, the ambulance will arrive on any summons and provide emergency treatment without any request to see insurance credentials. This does not mean, however, that treatment is free to this category of student. An explicit statement should be made to them as to their personal responsibility in this matter. In addition, the level of charge for dentists, opticians, medically related services (such as physiotherapy) and prescriptions should be clearly explained.

The funding of the NHS has been subject to a number of changes over the last years and the establishment of hospital trusts can mean that the willingness or ability of the local hospital to provide treatment for certain conditions, sometimes known as pre-existing conditions, varies from region to region. The position continues to remain somewhat obscure. It is unlikely, for instance, that a hospital would charge for care contingent on a pre-existing condition of pregnancy for the mother, but huge sums have been expended on perinatal care for the sick infant and this has been the subject of debate. Students, too, who arrive in the UK knowing that they have severe, chronic conditions or continuing acute illnesses may be sent bills for expensive or prolonged medical treatment. This section is not intended to question the rights or wrongs of the present system, simply as a recommendation that all international students have sufficient, clearly written advisory documentation to learn what the position is and what contingency plans they need to make. This can be reinforced during the welcome programme and additional advice offered in specific cases, preferably through the institution's own GP practice.

The GP/local doctor/general practitioner

The relationship between the institution and the local practice and hospital will help to determine the level of medical care and advice that the student community receives. The institution which includes a GP practice as one of its campus facilities is fortunate because it is able to provide healthcare as part of a holistic approach to welfare. The medical specialist can be clearly seen as part of the total service, offering conventional clinical care, together with advice on lifestyle and health education and, as far as confidentiality allows, proper networking with the whole management structure of the student support service. This relationship is certainly not impossible to achieve with off-campus GP facilities, but it is harder to secure and maintain and needs greater commitment from both the institution and the surgery. The doctors and medical staff, too, who spend most of their working day with the students and the institutional community, naturally become expert in those conditions most likely to affect the community. All this indicates that perhaps in this area more than in many others, the institution needs to work with the medical profession and clear any advisory documentation with them.

As medical practitioners and laymen, too, come to realize how closely mind and body are related, there is an increasing awareness of the role of the institution's GP surgery in the overall international student support system. Home sickness, anxiety, isolation and culture shock can all present symptoms of headaches, sore throats or digestive problems and the doctor and nurses who understand the institution's policy and its full provisions can often counsel students more successfully. The extent of the welfare net allows choice, and therefore some international students will select, even subconsciously, the warm authority of the practice nurse in preference to the religious adviser, or the international officer, or the counsellor or tutor. Some institutions choose to employ practice nurses directly, others approach the position differently. By whatever route, the service needs to be resourced in order to recognize and provide this, and be sufficiently integrated into the institution to have staff with the knowledge, skills and willingness to do so.

Using the system appropriately

The provision of female medical staff in an institution that wishes to recruit students from Muslim countries is vital. The ideal regime is one offering a choice, and male and female doctors and male and female nurses in particular for international students but, failing this, a female doctor should be available. If the institution does not directly employ the staff in the GP unit, it has less influence on the selection of personnel. A return will be made to this topic when discussing the role of the medical service for the spouse and family of the international student. This is a complex and sensitive issue and the institution may wish to make some assumptions in setting up the family scheme. One of these is that generally it is the husband who is the registered student and the possessor of the better education and the higher linguistic skills. It is the often the case, too, that wives may be accustomed to receiving support from an extended family or indeed from staff or servants in the care of children, and often for their own health matters. They may well have come from countries where a GP system does not exist, and therefore be unacquainted with the need for referrals through the GP or the role of the casualty department. For some, too, this is exposure to a better equipped and resourced system than they have ever seen for general access. These may be generalizations, and already liable to change, but the issues that arise from them create some of the greatest irritations or friction. It is, therefore, very worthwhile for the institution in the interests of both international student awareness and reduction of tension with local surgeries and hospitals to make clear the guidelines by which the system works. This again can be reaffirmed in the welcome package and through the other agencies which are working with international spouses and families.

These guidelines for the UK might include the following facts:

- It is unlikely that anyone in the GP practice will have adequate knowledge of the family first language. The bilingual partner (often the husband) therefore needs to accompany the family or seek translation assistance in advance. Some institutions have worked with their medical colleagues to provide mother tongue notes on key issues, but this does not compensate for the absence during the consultation of a fluent interpreter. There has been discussion, too, on the need for a leaflet in a number of languages listing the most common complaints and their medical remedies but the dangers of mistranslation or misinterpretation make this a very onerous task only to be undertaken by professional translators. Understandably, the medical profession has not given this a high priority, partly because leaflets have a very limited life span and application.
- Referrals to specialists and consultants are only made through the GP. It is not sensible to arrive in a hospital specialist clinic without an appointment, or a letter of referral.
- Casualty and accident and emergency departments exist for crises and the treatment of life-threatening conditions. They should not be attended for ailments or injuries which can be handled by the GP or the surgery nurse in a routine way.
- GPs are not an elastic resource which can immediately fulfil every patient's needs at any time of the day or night. Surgery hours exist to facilitate the care of the maximum number of patients with non-acute conditions. They should be used accordingly and GPs should not be summoned for trivial reasons out of surgery hours, and especially in the middle of the night.

- While every attempt is made to provide the patients with a choice of male or female GP or nurse, there may be occasions when this is not possible. Care should be taken to avoid this in the case of women but male students should be reminded of the equal professional competence of the female doctor and women of the objectivity of the male practitioner.

The above may appear negative or daunting. It should, therefore, be accompanied by a written assurance that it is intended that the best medical care available should be offered to all equally. Fears and anxieties, particularly with regard to young children, should always be communicated to the medical staff.

Contingency planning

No matter how excellent this provision, most institutions will at some stage have to face other issues in their concern for international students' health and welfare. The first is a simple one but proper arrangements will ease the difficulties. There are a number of illnesses and injuries that do not require hospitalization and, after they have been treated, would normally be managed in a non-clinical environment. Such an environment often means 'home'. The student with chicken pox or, flu or a broken leg would not expect in-patient medical care, but would require a degree of support. This could be provided through an in-patient insurance scheme that allows the student in-patient care in the institution's clinic, if it has one. It could equally be provided by family, and normally the student would elect to go home. This is less feasible for international students whose homes are often several thousand miles away. The location of responsibility for this care should be considered and the support services plugged into it. The Warden in the residence, the nurse, the counsellor, the student peer-pairing scheme may all have a role to play as well, of course, as the network of friends. It is advisable for the institution to have systems in place that can manage this.

A far more serious issue is the handling of terminal illness, or death of an international student. Although this is a rare event, it is of its nature traumatic and sudden and contingency plans are necessary so that uncertainty and confusion do not exacerbate distress. The requirement for medical confidentiality means that not all the information which the institution would like to have is always available. A trusting relationship between the institution and the GP will ensure that the best possible communication with the hospital is assured. There are diseases of which the institution believes it should be informed in the interests of the safety of the wider community. There should be clear points of contact both for information of this kind and within the institution whenever the death of a student occurs. The absolute necessity of this for international students is obvious. The next of kin of the international student may be thousands of miles away, to be reached only by poor communications. Arrangements have to be made, and the hospital may wrongly believe that these can be made by the next of kin. Sometimes they are not fluent in English, often they do not understand the relevant procedures and frequently money for travel or transport becomes a real issue. The institution should be in a position to satisfy itself that, in the rare cases where this occurs, it can handle contact with the Embassy, arrangements to meet religious or other requirements for the proper committal of the body and supportive grieving procedures for the student's family and friends within the student community. In the event that death arises from a communicable disease, there must be a plan, too, for sensitive counselling, diagnosis and preventative treatment for suspected contacts.

At the point of writing this, there is yet further discussion on legislation that may be passed to exclude most international students from the NHS system. The issue at present is only a matter for debate but it indicates the level of awareness that institutions need to acquire in health provision and the considerable advantages arising from a close relationship with the GPs who will be responsible for the healthcare of the international students. The NHS provisions are one of the UK marketing strengths overseas and this emphasizes again how often marketing advantage and real student care exactly coincide

Religious observance

The United Kingdom is a country with a Head of State who is also head of the established church, yet only a small proportion of the population are regular church goers. It has a traditional and predominantly Christian culture – some say in a post-Christian society. It is also a country which promotes complete freedom of religious worship. This is being stated here because it is easy to fall into the trap of assuming that nationality indicates religion in relation to international students, or of believing that all *members* of a religion are equally devout *practitioners* of it. Not all Arab students are Muslims, not all Ghanaian students are Christians, not all Filipino students are active Catholics. While the institutions must make provision for religious worship and observance, they should do so sensitively and in an informed manner. Formalized worship is of more importance to some religions than to others. Institutions should, therefore, be aware of the religious backgrounds of their students and be prepared to offer, as far as is reasonable, the facilities to support their respective beliefs. If it is out of the question to provide a purpose-built prayer room, ladies' room and ablution facilities for Muslim students then the details of the nearest mosque should be available on arrival. If it is impossible to provide halal or hillel meat, then the location of the closest retail outlet should be published. There should be some understanding of Ramadan and the implications of fasting and late night meals. While it is not expected that food and drink should be kept out of sight in the day time, there must be consideration of the physical stresses that the later stages of Ramadan can impose.

In order to gain a necessary insight into the major religions to which international students belong, it is helpful to have the services of consultants who can work with the regular chaplaincy. In the larger institutions, priest, rabbi and imam can ideally enrich one another's understanding and ecumenical vision. In the smaller ones, contacts with the local synagogue, temple or mosque can prove helpful. There are occasions, however, when the provision of centres for religious worship in the institution is not beneficial. In most cases the students are delighted that their religion is recognized and integrated, and considerable time and effort is saved by them in travelling. In a few instances, however, such a focus can mean that the absence at common prayer time of the less dedicated is noticed and that the centre can be used as a centre for feelings of a more political or racist than religious nature. Any institution making arrangements to offer rooms for religious adherence may be advised to do so on a licence basis which is renewable by the institution to the group annually or biannually. It should be made clear too that a room for prayer is not the same as a mosque or temple, and not always suitable for full religious rites such as those of death or marriage. The institution needs to have sufficient knowledge and interest to lay down rules for use of the facility and to convey them clearly and carefully to the student community. It is also sometimes the case that the use of the facility is not restricted to international students. There is a growing 'home' interest in Islam, Buddhism and other non-Western traditional religions.

Naturally, good communication between the institution and the student religious group is important in avoiding conflict. If there is an Islamic Committee which is responsible for the running and conduct of the prayer room under licence, and that Committee believes that the institution is caring and supportive, then anxieties about the emergence of fundamentalist groups or about the use of the room by outsiders, or for secular purposes, can be discussed frankly. The provision of a new prayer room carpet or of halal meat in central catering outlets can be negotiated if the parties have a respect for one another. Many international students come from countries whose main religion is Islam and that religion is quite specific about forms of worship and other requirements. It is natural, therefore, that the institution will be more conscious of the needs of this group, such as prayer rooms, single-sex residences and culinary requirements, than they might be of those of other groups. Sikhs, Hindus, Buddhists, Taoists, Jews also form part of the institution and that institution, if it offers a place of worship, normally provides a Christian ecumenical one. Jewish students sometimes seek hillel house facilities and some institutions provide them. Kosher meals are often difficult to organize through central catering outlets, as are halal. Orthodox Jews have much the same acculturation problems of working and travelling on the Sabbath as Muslims do in being surrounded by their peer group, eating and drinking during Ramadan.

The devoutly religious will have considered all these factors before they decide to travel overseas. The full range of facilities available should be explained to them before arrival and again during the welcome package. Students recognize that compromise often has to be made and they will normally respond favourably and flexibly if they have access to all the necessary information and feel that they are joining a liberal and unprejudiced community that tolerates all sincerely held beliefs. Needless to say, those responsible for student welfare within the institution will have as a key concern the creation of an open atmosphere. Bigotry or racial hatred expressed within the institution will be regarded as offensive and contrary to the institutional code of conduct. In spite of this, it is sometimes the case that there has to be a degree of security concerning the disclosure of the names of members of religious societies. This confidentiality of data is especially important in the fraught world of religious and national tensions.

Religious observance is a far-reaching topic, and additional information on diet, single-sex residences, the protection of women and sports facilities can be found in other sections.

Family support

As has been mentioned before, an increasing number of international students, particularly at postgraduate level, are being accompanied overseas by their spouses and families. If the institution believes that a happy and secure student is likely to be academically more successful than one less well supported, then thought and resourcing will have to be applied to the care and acculturation of the entire family.

There has been much debate on whether a student performs better if he or she is separated from the family and so concentrates exclusively on academic work, speaks English all the time instead of first language in the evenings and at weekends and generally focuses on completing the programme and returning home. What is incontrovertible is that the student whose family is in the UK, and to whom he or she returns every night, is handicapped by a family whose members are feeling isolated, neglected, inadequate or victimized.

Integrating the family

Family housing has already been discussed, as has family medical care. Beyond this, the integration of the family is best assisted by the provision of a 'friend' to whom the family may turn, by schooling for the children, support for wives with pre-school children and assistance with acquiring English language competence. At some stage all of these desiderata come together.

Educational institutions are part of the wider community and, through a network of staff families and their contacts, it is possible to create a pool of volunteers to run a family link scheme. It is helpful if the organization of this is located within the institution, perhaps as part of the English language centre, the chaplaincy, the student support office or the international office. On arrival, international postgraduates and their families can be linked to local families who are interested in meeting and helping to integrate those from overseas. They do not only provide opportunities for friendship, but also explain shopping facilities, give advice on clothing and climate, engage with the children, allow the whole family to practise their English and to share their own culture with a host family. When the link scheme works well, it is valuable to both parties, with the host family acquiring knowledge and appreciation of a culture beyond their own and the overseas family being provided with insights into the real way of life in that country and an experience of affection and warmth beyond that extended by 'professional carers'. Any one wishing to help has something to offer. Those with young children can immediately identify with overseas young parents; those whose children are grown up and away can become surrogate grandparents and aunts. So many international students value being part of a real home and welcome the opportunity to discuss issues of interest beyond the purely academic.

Other volunteers may be trained to teach English to spouses. Much has been said in previous sections of the dilemma of the spouse, particularly if he or, generally, she comes from a culture where informal mixing of the sexes is not permitted. Female volunteers can be organized for conversational English teaching, one to one, in the home of the student's spouse if that is desired. Groups of mothers, too, can be organized which allow conversational English, companionship and shared childcare. Some institutions already have crèches, pre-school playgroups or mother and toddler groups. If they are not provided by the institution, then their absence allows opportunity for interaction with the wider community. Provided the mother is sufficiently fluent in English or is accompanied by someone who is, these visits to 'outside' childcare facilities offer a broader experience of living abroad. If the husband is prepared to allow it, the institution can also organize or facilitate a number of activities for the family. It is necessary, however, to gain the trust and understanding of the husband who should, in the beginning, be used as a channel for all communication on family activities.

Children and schooling

Children of school age, almost without exception, find the British primary school a stimulating and supportive environment and the progress of a happy 5-year-old in second language acquisition is amazing. Institutional help is normally sought in finding a school, and advice should be available on catchment areas, free schooling and the British school culture. This advice should include the fact that students coming for a very limited period are not entitled to enjoy free schooling for their children and that children of international students who are over 16 years old are not necessarily entitled to free schooling. Where the institution habitually registers a large number of international students with children, it is helpful to make contact with the local primary and secondary schools and provide them with details of the nationality and background of the international students and the expected trend in recruitment. Some schools have responded so positively that they provide mother tongue literature for new families and mother and child clubs for out-of-school activities.

Such sharing of responsibility for the student family welfare by the wider community is always welcomed by the institution. The importance of the Greenaway Report lies in its affirmation of the financial significance of international student recruitment to the local and national economy. While the academic community, including of course the students, can do its utmost to ensure freedom from racism, bigotry or abuse in its own community, it is only through relationships with the wider community that it can explain its role in the whole venture of international education. If those who work in, and who send their children to, the local schools have first-hand knowledge of Turkish toddlers or Japanese adolescents they are less likely to complain when local housing stock is occupied by international families. The wider community includes the Rotary Club, the wives' group, the parents' associations, the neighbourhood schemes and the local churches.

Recreation

Contacts made naturally and friendships developed for a common interest are among the happiest outcomes of activity-based clubs and societies. Students' Unions in most cases will devote effort and resourcing to the establishment of interest groups which include a host of sporting activities, pastimes, recreational societies, cultural groups and almost any excuse for two or three like-minded students to gather together! The institution will usually provide sporting facilities but the students will organize, manage and inspire the teams and individuals that use them. In this forum, international students can experience total integration and acceptance with a common language and an enthusiasm that overcomes all difficulties of oral communication and cultural bias. Little needs to be done by the institution in these circumstances and non-intervention is a successful strategy. Some assistance may be necessary to ensure that Muslim women students have access to a single-sex session at the institution's pool or that some keep-fit classes also offer such sessions. The institution can point the way in stimulating the creation of an international student society, which should act as a social and cultural focus for international students and as the umbrella organization for national societies or regional interest groups. These are beneficial as long as they support the identity of the international student without separating him or her too far from the prevailing British culture and context. Any classification which stresses those things that separate and divide – not only from the host culture but also one nation from another – is undesirable and unfortunate. National societies can be encouraged to be open and welcoming, celebrating cultural heritage – not exclusive, judgmental or xenophobic. Security in one's own identity can often lead to greater

acceptance of another's, and this should be one of the key objectives of the international and the national societies.

Additional support

Much of the foregoing has dealt with the additional dimension
required for international student support which is built into existing structures. Many other services fall into this category and need
only a brief mention here. The expectation of the institution is that
such services offer the level of support to international students that
is available for all students, but that in addition they recognize the
particular issues and needs that face international students. Counsellors will be aware that some overseas cultures find it alien to
share feelings with others, even with a professional, non-judgmental
listener. The discussion of emotions, sexuality, inadequacy or self-
doubt is not something to which they are accustomed and a special
tenacity and sensitivity will be needed to reach them and to work
with them. Problems of home sickness and identity crises may also
be more severe than for home students. Student advisers may be
available for all students, but provision may still be made for an
international student adviser who will offer the institution's expertise on issues of immigration, visas, work permits and employment
and Home Office legislation. The circumstances relating to, and problems of, visa issue should not be underestimated. They are for obvious reasons concerns both for marketing and student care. Much
discussion has taken place between the institutions and the government on UK visa regulations and the difficulties relating to international student recruitment. UKCOSA has considerable expertise
in this area and has made advice available both to institutions and
to potential students. The British Council has become involved in
dialogue with the Immigration Department over procedures and
schedules. While the legitimate concerns of government and citizens
as to carefully regulated entry must be recognized, there must also
be an appreciation of the efforts being made by the institutions to
secure well-qualified students.

The international student adviser role can grow so that it becomes
the focus of welfare support and concern for international students,
with responsibility for management of, and liaison with, all the
activities and provisions enumerated in this chapter. The location
of such a role whether in the student support service, in the Dean
of Students' office, in the Students' Union, or in the International
Office is a matter for the institution. Wherever the post or posts
are placed, considerable collaboration is required with the other

offices. One of the advantages of the incorporation of this post in the International Office is the statement that the institution makes in so doing: that the care of its existing international students and the marketing directed at potential international students are seen as indivisible and mutually supportive.[2]

The Careers Office will also offer care for all students but will recognize particular requirements of the non-UK student. Often international students will have had a career path mapped out for them and indeed the cost of and planning for study overseas will have shaped and sharpened their concentration on the choice of profession. Many international students, for the same reasons, will be following vocational courses and often the manpower planning requirements of their countries and sponsors will have been expressed clearly before departure. More and more often, however, national companies and multinational corporations are aware of the reservoir of talent and intellect of international students in the host institutions, either available to relocate in other countries or to return home with multicultural experience and knowledge. Such companies direct their enquiries to the Careers Office, and so Careers Officers often organize recruitment fairs aimed at multinational employers. With the internet and website availability, employment opportunities are becoming easier to access and publicize. The Careers Officers in the institutions of higher education are the professionals from which the international students gain information as to the next phase of opportunity open to them. Similarly, student counsellors and advisers in schools or FE colleges can give guidance to international students as they complete UCAS forms or look for further opportunities abroad or at home.

Academic support

Whatever the institution offers in the way of support and care, it is intended only that this should complement the quality of relationship that should exist between teacher and learner, between supervisor and researcher or between lecturer and student. The student is attending an institution of learning, and nothing can compensate if the quality of the learning interaction fails. Much has been written of the special relationship between those who teach and those who learn. At one time it was believed to be almost sacred; it has been enshrined in law as having special responsibility and status. Heloise and Abélard may seem a long way from distance learning but, whether in ivy clad college or portakabin classroom, the learning relationship is central to student happiness and success.

The student whose tutor provides enlightened feedback on work submitted, or the researcher whose supervisor invites him home for Sunday lunch is most unlikely to complain about photocopying restrictions or lack of lab space. Conversely, students who feel that those who teach them have no genuine interest in them complain about everything and even the most excellent support facilities can only ameliorate the position. The expectations, the vulnerabilities and the objectives of international students make these issues even more acute for them. Some discussion on teaching methods has been offered in Chapter 2, and institutional awareness will be considered in Chapter 5. It is sufficient to say at this stage that if the teaching relationship is right, then the support services can work to reinforce a very positive experience. If it is not, the support services can only struggle to make it acceptable. The provision of excellent and comprehensive welfare services may mean that academic staff assume they have been relieved of all responsibility for their students' welfare. This is a dilemma for the institution. It was never intended that academic staff should secure accommodation for their students, but it is hoped that they will be alert to accommodation difficulties being experienced by them. It is not intended that they should take the place of professional counsellors, but it is hoped that they will be sufficiently in touch with a tutorial group to recognize when a student is in need of help. Indeed, they could even be the first to provide it.

Quality mechanisms now provide a number of advisers as part of the quality assurance procedures in higher education. Research students do now receive a more structured and monitored package than was previously the case. All this works to the advantage both of the international student and the home student. It may be satisfactory to work with a brilliant academic holding an international reputation in the field, but if that academic also recognizes that the student may need support and friendship outside the narrow academic area, then the student – and the institution – is fortunate indeed.

Course completion

The student has moved to successful completion of the course and is turning attention to the next phase of his or her life. As the institution has welcomed and acculturated its international students, so it should mark their leaving and prepare them for another phase.

Interesting debates have taken place on the need for reorientation and the benefits that arise from it. Reorientation can take place during one half day, when a programme combining practical assistance and guided exercises can be offered. The practical assistance can include information on packing and shipping firms, details of the alumni associations and information on scholarships for further study. A guided fantasy[3] should be led by someone experienced in counselling and must be conducted gently and sensitively. It is not intended as a psychotherapy session but as a safe and supportive vehicle from which students can look realistically at what they are leaving and to what they are about to return. They should be led to acknowledge that change will have taken place, both within themselves and in the country and the people to whom they will be returning. Some may not have returned home for the whole of their stay overseas; others may have returned as visitors with all the excitement and glamour that a short visit entails. Now they return to take up responsibilities in the family and in the work place, and both they and those they care for will have altered during their period abroad. Students should be invited to participate and encouraged to evaluate the experience.

The institution should be aware too that not all students will be available for the formal end of the programme. Many postgraduate students are unable to return for graduation. Like the British, many cultures place emphasis on formality and ceremony and the leaving of the institution should be marked as a rite of passage. Completing A Level students, as much as departing PhDs, can enjoy some formal entertainment and farewell, whether over tea with the student welfare adviser or lunch with the Pro-Vice-Chancellor. Again, this provides the institution with an opportunity to emphasize the bond between student and institution and to distribute data on alumni groups and national contacts. Traditionally, graduates have been welcomed into lifelong membership of the university community, and this kind of association can be offered to students in all types of institution. Some university institutions have developed the practice of holding graduation ceremonies overseas in order to allow the maximum number of their students to graduate in person. If degrees are conferred on such occasions the full panoply of ceremonial may be required and this is, even in abbreviated form, expensive and labour-intensive. It is, however, often considered real evidence of commitment to the graduand and to the sponsor. Other ceremonies may offer a celebration of the degree rather than its conferment and these can be more relaxed in style and less demanding in terms of personnel and protocol.

The following chapter will discuss the role of the alumni association and the concept of continuing care. Again, it is an example of the mutual benefit to student and institution. The students are offered continuing communication and support when they return home, and the institution knows that it has increasingly influential ambassadors committed to maintaining its reputation for excellence across the world.

Conclusion

From the moment that he or she writes to the institution for information, the international applicant, student and alumnus should be aware that he or she is regarded as important – primarily as a human being, but also as a customer. Nothing written here suggests that this should not be the case for the home student. It is, however, recognized that international students have particular needs and vulnerabilities and bring with them particular commercial and financial benefits. It is hypocritical to deny their value as customers, but no worthwhile support system could be effective on that basis alone. Where there is real concern for the individual and genuine appreciation of the inestimable rewards of cross-cultural integration, then the support services will be inspired to offer a dimension beyond the academic. In this context, problems can become issues and difficulties can be seen as challenges.

Endnotes

1 The United Kingdom Council for Overseas Student Affairs (UKCOSA) is in the forefront of such organizations.
   Their role has been discussed in an earlier chapter but this chapter cannot be written without further comment on the advances that they have pioneered and consolidated in student care. Their conferences, training programmes, advice sessions and research have moved the profession forward. Their recent literature survey on international students in the UK and their seminar report, *Contrasting Approaches to International Education: Views from around the World* (Sharples 1997), indicates the scope and depth of their expertise. They not only offer practical skills and advice but also stimulating discussion on the concept of the international student.
   The following concluding comments from the UKCOSA seminar report on 'contrasting approaches to international education' are by Steve Sharples, Assistant Director, Research and Development, UKCOSA:

   The notion of international education as an economic product, notably through the recruitment of international students, . . . raises a number of important issues . . . It must be recognised that all education per se is culture-bound. It is both an expression of that culture and one of the primary instruments used for transmitting cultural values. The question must be asked, therefore, whether it is even appropriate to pursue a vigorous export strategy in the first place. The gap between what is inherently good about domestic provision and the needs of the 'foreign' consumer must be bridged, and resolving this dilemma is at the very heart of international education.

(Sharples 1997: 41)

2 The idea of the virtuous circle is outlined in Chapter 5 and stresses the interrelationship of learning, caring and spending as the basis of the institutional strategy for internationalization.

3 A typical programme might be run over half a day towards the close of the academic year and conclude with refreshments. A suggested structure might be:

- A welcome to the event by a senior colleague representing the institution.
- Brief talks on practical topics such as removal firms and freight carriers and the advantages of membership of the institution's Graduate Association.
- Sessions in groups with feedback on looking back – memories of the period of study in the UK (good and bad) and looking forward – anticipation of the return home.
- A qualified and experienced colleague should be responsible for the guided fantasy which can be rooted in questions or feelings on departure and anxieties, as well as excitement, about the return.
- A relaxing transitional period for summing up, completion of evaluation forms, shared enjoyment of refreshments.

5

MARKET CONSOLIDATION: MAKING THE MOST OF INTERNAL AND EXTERNAL RESOURCES

Introduction

There has never been any doubt that once a market has been investigated, personal contact with that market has led to more effective and speedy market penetration. There is little doubt, either, that comprehensive and caring student support helps to ensure the successful outcome, which is essentially 'repeat sales'. The third factor, which needs to be effectively managed, is that of market consolidation. This can, for ease, be divided under the headings of cash and communication, and in many respects these are interdependent.

Resourcing – cash

The resourcing of any project is fundamental to its success. The debate on the level of resourcing most appropriate to international recruitment is complicated by the somewhat unusual circumstances of at least the majority of the UK participants. Language schools and some independent schools and colleges may be able to create income that will generate 'profit'. The public sector institutions, however, work to create 'surplus'. Since there are no shareholders or dividend-benefiting directors in these institutions any surplus belongs to the institution, and is ploughed back into the institutional facilities and development programme. Financial success in international recruitment, therefore, redounds to the benefit of the entire community. The fact that this is not, and should not be, the sole reason for embarking on it has been discussed in earlier chapters, as has the danger of too great a dependency upon it.

In any budget the analysis of vulnerability will be important and, at the time of writing, few UK institutions at any level, and of whatever size, will be untouched by the economic problems in South East Asia. When the government introduced full-cost fees, the underlying rationale was that the existing system should not subsidize the service and products offered to the international student. That being the case, the amount generated by international student fees should be the maximum amount that can be expended on these students. It is, of course, the hope of the institution that the fees collected considerably exceed the amount directly expended on the international community and thus create a surplus which will, of necessity, be expended on the whole community, of which the international student is a part. This ideal outcome is, therefore, to everyone's advantage.

The real 'cost' of international student education, however, must include calculations relating to the whole recruitment activity. While it is possible to believe that appropriately qualified students from overseas would arrive at the door without any promotional activity, there is little evidence to support this hypothesis. It is increasingly clear that UK institutions are in competition with one another for the most appropriate of the home students.[1] One only has to consider the quality of the prospectus, or the activities of the Schools Liaison Office, or the energetic planning of the Graduate School to be convinced of that. When the competition is not only from the UK, but also from a number of overseas 'players', and when the student and sponsor are taking so much more expensive and far-reaching life decisions, it is understandable that more effective and persuasive practices may have to be used. Many of these have already been identified, and the institution must be clear how far it is prepared to invest in the process and, as a corollary to that, the quality of the marketing with which it wishes to be associated. Some of these direct costs are identified below and some will be evident as indirect costs in the later discussion on communication and structures.

The British Council membership subscription

The role of the British Council, and particularly the ECS, has been considered earlier. Its success in that role can be evidenced by the numbers of UK institutions which now consider its subscription as vital to their marketing portfolio and indeed to the success of UK plc. It is to be frequently re-emphasized – and this is not always immediately acceptable to any individual institution – that one element in marketing must be the reinforcement of the reputation of the UK as a whole as a provider of a quality educational product. Institutional success is likely to be short-term if the reputation of the national product is tarnished. There are now 286 members of ECS[7] paying annual subscriptions of between £6000 and £18,000 a year. While Oxford and Cambridge have now and then elected to go their own way outside ECS for obvious reasons, they are now included in membership, as are most of the higher educational institutions. A significant number of FE colleges are included, together with most of the independent schools and many of the private ELT (English Language Teaching) providers. It is not the task of this book to represent the advantages of ECS membership but it is clear that most of the institutions with a real long-term commitment to international recruitment have decided to opt into ECS. This, however, is not all that the British Council offers and requires! In some countries, such as Japan, they established a Japan Club with a limited number of subscribing members. This additional subscription allowed British Council Tokyo to employ an additional member of staff who would be dedicated to Club activities. This avoided the undesirable alternative of all subscribers subsidizing the activities of a few institutions. It also allowed a limited number of institutions to run a pilot, and to commit themselves to an expensive and long-term market. The subscribers inside and out of the Japan Club will have a view on its effectiveness and value for money. More developments along these lines may be considered, with institutions opting into activity in certain geographical or subject areas. Inclusion may require an additional subscription.

While ECS membership provides advantages, such as market surveys and *Marketing News*[3] and preferential inclusion in British Council-organized exhibitions, it does not offer free participation in these exhibitions. Institutions who wish to have a market presence and choose the medium of the exhibition will have to budget not only for travel, accommodation and freight but also for the levy or ratchet required by the exhibition organizer, whether private/commercial or the British Council. One benefit of British Council exhibition organization is the return of all 'surplus' to the overall enterprise. Excess income made by large-volume participations in successful exhibitions in, for example, Malaysia, will provide a surplus expended at the discretion of the Board[4] perhaps on additional market surveys or on a marketing post in a less developed region. If the average exhibition levy is about £600[5] and an institution plans to attend ten a year, then membership and exhibition overheads alone will require a budget of about £16,000 for the medium-sized institution. These costs are absolutely basic and do not include any related to travel or overseas subsistence for exhibition attendance.

Travel and related expenses

Purchasing the travel package

It is obvious that if the institution is to be seen overseas then arrangements have to be made for selected staff to travel to the various venues and to remain there while the business is conducted. This includes, but is certainly not restricted to, exhibition attendance. The rules and procedures for travel expenditure vary between institutions according to resource, institutional ethos and often timing. Those responsible for the budget should know the institutional practice in all of these areas. Does the institution 'shop around' or place all its orders through one or two nominated travel companies as recommended by a central procurement or purchase office? The advantages of the former include the cheap bucket shop fare and the holiday package. The advantage of the latter includes consistency and high-quality service assured for a valued, high-order customer and often 'bonus' paid to the institution for volume traffic. The internal auditor may require that all travel paid for by the institution is booked by the institution and not the individual. On the other hand, an over-pressed, smaller institution may be grateful if the individual travellers make their own ticketing arrangements.

Traveller safety

Whatever the procedure, the institution will wish to be certain that if it invites or requires its employees to travel for the benefit of the institution then the safest and most sensible arrangements that can be made are made. This will include, wherever possible, selecting reputable airlines, ensuring that visas are obtained where necessary and that proper insurance is secured. Needless to say, colleagues should not be required to travel to any area where there is evidence of 'clear and present danger'. While the exigencies of terrorism are beyond the predictions of even the most caring institution, judicious monitoring of the FCO web page[6] can at least ensure that the International Office, or whoever is making the arrangement, is informed as to the current position. Proper checking on visas is essential and the most expensive and important visit can be cancelled or curtailed by the lack of the necessary paperwork, either for the airport of departure or the overseas point of immigration. Responsible travel agents will give advice on visas but often state it is the individual's responsibility to check on this advice. Even the most eminent and innocent colleagues can be rejected at the entry point or, at best, submitted to difficult and time-consuming questioning.

Insurance

The provision of high-quality and high-cost insurance is a matter for the institution, but those planning the budget should be aware of the expenditure and those responsible for the oversight of travel should ensure that as comprehensive a package as possible is available to the traveller. While it is essential that it covers the lost suitcase at JFK or Charles de Gaulle or the doctor's bills in Delhi, it is also possible to include air ambulance cover, which is important if colleagues are being asked to work in areas with less developed and accessible medical facilities.[7] Cover can be extended to include flights for replacement staff, which might be needed in the case of serious or prolonged illness at a critical event. No institution will wish to dwell on the eventualities that all who send colleagues on overseas visits must have in the backs of their minds. Insurance can cover kidnap policies, which can be quickly and discreetly arranged for specific missions in specific areas as can the return of bodies to the home country. The institution's regular policy for its employees will cover serious and permanent injury and death in service. All of this should be checked at an early phase in the establishment of an overseas recruitment policy. Once established, it is hoped that it will never be needed. Individual colleagues when travelling will appreciate some documentation to indicate the named insurance company and contact points in case of need. In addition to insurance cover it is important that travellers receive advice on vaccinations and prophylactics. Again, this can be accessed through the web[8] or through the GP. It would be customary for the institution to pay for various necessary inoculations and tablets such as anti-malarials. It has been common, too, for travellers to some parts of the world to carry sterile anti-HIV kits containing clean needles and sutures. More extensive kits containing plasma are available for travellers to more inaccessible areas but such areas are not often the location of British Council exhibitions.

Flights and accommodation

Most of the areas which provide the greatest numbers of students are at least 8000 miles from the UK and so long-haul travel has become a necessity. The institution will have a policy on who travels how.

- Does the Dean need to be booked in business class?
- Does the business class concession extend to all long-haul travellers?
- Is there to be a rest day on arrival for long-haul travellers who fly economy?
- How will the long-haul traveller proceed from the UK airport to his or her home?
- Some commercial companies now refuse to allow employees to drive themselves after long flights across time zones. If this is the case, what arrangements can be made?

All these questions need to be answered before any accurate budget can be drawn up.

The institution must also decide on a policy for overseas accommodation and hospitality. Many exhibition organizers negotiate special rates for exhibition hotels and often British Council offices or UK Embassies and High Commissions can arrange for accommodation in the 'preferred' hotel at preferential rates. In some countries, there is little in the way of hotels between the famous multinational five star chains and fairly insalubrious and doubtful 'local' accommodation. In others, the full range of facilities and prices is available and sensible judgement has to be made. Again, there will be an institutional view as to where it is appropriate for the head of the institution or senior management to stay and what is the minimum acceptable for any traveller. There are occasions, too, when travellers on the institution's behalf may include students. The consideration to be borne in mind is the impression that the institution wishes to make and the working conditions for the traveller. It may seem inappropriate in a developing country for travellers to be accommodated with some show of affluence, but it is essential in these countries that the traveller has access to direct dial telephones, faxes and English-speaking assistance. It is important for his or her safety that the kitchens reach a minimum standard, that the water served is bottled and the taxis called to the hotel are secure. It is also useful if the safe deposit works, or indeed exists, and if there is a facility for confirming onward airline tickets and taking telephone messages. These are the minima required for the traveller who is not only undertaking the marketing activity but also quite frequently trying to maintain some contact with and commitment to work back in the office.

Encouragement to travel

There are occasions when the minimum is not enough and the institution needs to reflect its quality in the accommodation that it takes both for its staff and for its entertaining. If sponsors, students and families are met and interviewed in doubtful accommodation, it gives a clear and unfortunate message as to the standing of the UK institution and the priority that is accorded to international relations. If the budget only permits mediocre accommodation it might be better to hold interviews and meetings in British Council offices or at the sponsor's work place. On the other hand, it would seem inappropriate to be obviously expending large amounts of money on luxuries when the country itself is not affluent or when the individual students are obviously in need of financial support and scholarships. As always, an informed and sensitive judgement needs to be made and that judgement then costed and carried forward into the budget. There is a view that the cheaper the travel, the more often it can take place. There is also a view that it is better in the long term for travellers to be asked to exist in conditions which are more than acceptable and for the institution always to be represented in a manner that reflects its claim to quality.

The costs must also include a decision as to the 'encouragement' offered to staff whose job description may not require them to travel for recruitment purposes. There may well be some members of the team who are contracted to include travel and time spent abroad and the clauses in such contracts will have been accepted on appointment. However, for the vast majority of the colleagues who travel, this will involve additional work and new responsibilities. Those who accept this have the immeasurable benefit of exposure to new places, cultures, cuisines and peoples. This is generally acknowledged to be sufficient reason, together with institutional loyalty and an interest in professional and personal development, for enough members of staff to work overseas. In the climate of increasing assessment, of worsening SSRs and additional pressures to perform, it might prove necessary to budget for honoraria or for replacement teaching. The provision of good internal communication of corporate objectives, of clear direction from the management, of supportive help from those whose full-time responsibility is international recruitment and of an acceptable package relating to flights, pick-up and hotels, may make such additional payments unnecessary.

Above all, however, the traveller needs to believe that the institution values what he or she is doing, understands the considerable effort that is required to do it well, and will respond with real care and support in the event of difficulties. Not all of this can be costed but the confidence that it brings is beyond value.

Literature and information

Some attention has been paid in the section on exhibitions to the quality and spread of literature that is required. The generic term 'information' now includes websites, videos and CD-ROMS, as well as the more traditional hard copies.

Those preparing the budget need to have decided whether specific information is to be created for the overseas market or whether the existing package is sufficient. Some use of mother tongue insertions can be helpful and eye-catching. This is particularly significant in a country where English is not only a different language but a different script. Headlines in Arabic, Russian, Chinese and Japanese can be very worthwhile. Good quality translation and graphics are not cheap. In some institutions, fortunate in their existing overseas student community, students or alumni may agree to do this. In some cases, professional translators and typesetters may be desirable or necessary. Some institutions now have fonts or programmes which allow these languages to be produced as part of desktop publishing. Videos may be organized with mother tongue insertions or, more sensitively, with a focus on international students and their needs. Often, two video versions will need to be available – one of which will require careful attention to the cutting of pub scenes, mixed sunbathing or inappropriate dressing! Such a version could also show family housing, English language classes and the welcome programme. It is not surprising that the sponsor, committing something equivalent to £50,000 for a student to achieve a PhD in a technological discipline, will be more interested in the research quality and teaching excellence or reputation of the institution than in the nightlife available in the nearest city. On the other hand, no one subscribes to the view that overseas education is merely a training in a discipline or a set of skills, and video evidence of the availability of a full and rounded, yet secure, environment is persuasive. If additional or specific information on video or hard copy is required, it needs to be costed. It should be noted, too, that videos may need to be available in both the world formats – much use is now made of NTSC. Costing should include such small items as a visiting card in English and the relevant language, and 'flyers' and posters to promote the institution. These will be further considered as part of external communications.

Hospitality

The successful traveller should be in a position to accept and offer hospitality, both overseas and in the home institution. Many cultures are traditionally and innately generous and especially solicitous for the care and entertainment of visitors. Such hospitality has created a lasting impression on the visitor and has perhaps changed the manner and the extent to which it is returned when at home. Often the institutional representative will receive overwhelming hospitality when travelling overseas from colleagues, potential students, families, British Council and alumni. It is good to be able to have the means to return this, either through the hotel in the overseas venue or, even better, back at home.

Any budget should allow for limited and properly accounted hospitality when overseas, and for appropriate and properly organized hospitality when at home. An increasing numbers of visitors arrive at UK institutions every week and the institution should have a code of practice for dealing with them and a section in the international budget which can accommodate this. Circumstances will vary but, in general, if the central office for international affairs is meeting the cost, it needs to know well in advance in order to contribute to the programme and to make some input into the contact. Often, the whole visit will be organized centrally. The hospitality offered should reflect the institution's style and the status of the visitors. It would seem sensible to offer visiting student groups refreshments in a student outlet, so that they can experience student amenities and meet existing students. It would also seem appropriate that a visiting rector is hosted, at least in part, by senior management and dined in a manner that further emphasizes the standing of both the institution and the visitor. This is not a recommendation for indulgent and lengthy lunches, and indeed most senior visitors have heavy programmes with clearly defined objectives. It is, however, an acknowledgement that the institution will wish to offer appropriate hospitality. Meals offered within the institution reduce time spent in local travel, allow another facet of the institution to be displayed, offer confidentiality, and keep the expenditure within the institutional coffers.

Western institutions have become accustomed to the habit of exchanging visiting cards. They are also becoming used to the pleasant but worrying custom of exchange of gifts. The questions raised by this custom include, to whom, what, when and how often? Some cultures, perhaps those to the east rather than to the west, place great value on this formality and perform it with grace and dignity. The institution has to decide how to return this generosity and budget for it. Gifts can carry the institutional logo, if they are to have a longer lasting significance. They should be appropriate in price, unisex if possible (to avoid giving lace handkerchiefs to the male Dean of Engineering), resonant of the geographical area, culturally acceptable (a cut-glass whisky goblet might be unsuitable for some Pakistanis) and transportable. This latter criterion not only relates to weight but also to passage through airport security. Lead crystal paperweights show up as unidentified heavy metal in the x-ray machine and letter openers cause real problems! In addition to all of this, they should be presented with dignity and given with grace. A list should be kept to avoid the embarrassment of a visitor receiving the same gift on a subsequent occasion. Some institutions now use wrapping paper which depicts the logo. For many cultures the manner in which the gift is wrapped will indicate the solemnity of the occasion. It is useful to know what the recipient's custom is for opening gifts in front of the donor. All of this, gift, wrap and package, has to be costed and included in a budget.

The acceptance of gifts must again be organized within the institution's codes of conduct. There may be a system for reporting gifts received and a log kept. The overriding requirement for the recipient institution is that any gift should not influence judgement, or secure unmerited advantage for the donor or benefit to any great extent the individual who is simply performing an institutional role. The size and nature of the gift is obviously a key factor in all of this. The institution may require disclosure of gifts over a certain value, perhaps £50, or of gifts given in unusual circumstances, such as on the eve of an examination, or when a student is seeking admission to the institution. If it is difficult to refuse or to return a gift genuinely offered in gratitude or friendship, it is always possible to accept it on behalf of the institution, to locate it centrally and even to donate it for student hardship causes at a later time.

Setting up offices overseas

If periodic presence in a country is believed to be valuable, then the extension of this idea to permanent presence should offer considerably greater value. For this reason, a number of the larger institutions have established, or are establishing, offices overseas. Twinning, validating and franchise activities have been discussed in an earlier chapter and all of these, with their need for quality control, benefit from the constant presence of the UK institution. This is not only an option for the larger or better established institutions. Groups of those less well resourced could combine to establish a base, or work out of a base, located through or next to a reputable and trusted agent.

Once the institution has decided on such a development, perhaps in the first instance to initiate or manage a specific non-recruitment activity, then the benefits will accrue to recruitment. If these are to be maximized, some provision needs to be made to run the office, to capitalize on marketing potential and cost-efficiency. This, too, will have to be budgeted. Stocks of materials have to be lodged in the office, PCs and databases set up, stationery organized and bilingual secretarial help secured. It is necessary, too, if the office is to be managed by a member of staff of the UK institution, to include appropriate housing and salary package (incorporating health cover, flights and related incidentals) in the costing. As with all these activities, it must be conducted with both a view to value for money and a regard for appropriate quality. An office in a bad location sends the wrong signals, as does one so well appointed that it seems out of place with educational objectives. The office can undertake school and higher education visits, counsel potential students, act as a focus for alumni activities in that city, staff exhibitions, respond to queries, run pre-departure briefings and generally offer accessible and immediate help and advice, both to the international market and to the host institution. This 'on the spot' interpretation of political, educational and economic trends is a valuable tool, as is the opportunity to follow up leads, to monitor developments at first hand and create and sustain links and networks.

The secondment or appointment of personnel, the setting up of the premises, the recruitment of local support staff, the freighting of literature and the funding of local travel, in-country or within the region, are all achieved at a cost. This cost must be recognized, provided for, controlled and evaluated if the scheme is to be successful. This out-posting of international activity should, in so far as it relates to the budget for international recruitment, be included in that budget so that accurate outcomes can be assessed and evaluated.

Scholarships

Setting the level of tuition fee

For some in the educational sector, the level of fees to be charged to international students is clearly a matter for their own judgement, based on the need to be competitive and an awareness of what the market will bear. Fees for ELT courses, or at some of the private schools and colleges, are set to make a profit while retaining long-term market share. In the UK, the FE institutions came onto the international arena at a later stage than the HE institutions and did so only when the hand of the LEA was removed. The institutions of higher education had, from the inception of full-cost fees until the early 1990s, the minimum level of tuition fees for international students set by government through the Department of Education and Science. The fees were set for cost bands[9] and were intended as full-cost fees, as indicated at the beginning of this chapter. It would be difficult to argue that one additional Taught Masters student in, for example, Computer Science, costs as much as one research student in, for example, Animal Husbandry, but that was the basis of the fee level and the banding. If all the indirect costs, many of which have not yet been discussed, were included this would probably be the case.

After some ten years of this direction, the UK government decided that institutions should set their own level of fee, opening up possibilities for undercutting one another or for making a case for quality reflected by the fee charged. Each year, institutions choose either to increase the level of fees by the rate of inflation or by more or less, and the position is now in 1998 one of considerable diversity within the disciplines and between the institutions. The debate on top-up home fees and the continuing agenda of differentiation between institutions and disciplines, together with the £1000 tuition fee, has only added more variables to this equation.

- Should popular subjects charge higher fees?
- Should subjects in less demand charge lower fees?
- Should countries in need be charged reduced fees?
- Should publicly sponsored students pay the same fees as private students?
- Should undergraduate and postgraduate courses in the same band charge the same fee?
- What can be covered by the tuition fee and what charged as extra?
- Should highly regarded institutions charge more than others less sought after?

All these and a number of other questions have now made the setting of the fee a difficult and important annual decision.

Funding the scholarship

This has been simplified to some extent by the use of the scholarship scheme. If the fee agreed as the institutional tuition fee is the gross fee that the institution charges, this can be ameliorated by scholarship funding being paid into the tuition fee account, resulting in a net fee levied on the student or sponsor. If a full scholarship is given by organizations outside the institution then the scholarship cost to the institution is zero (or at worst, zero plus the cost of attracting and maintaining the scholarship sponsor). If the scholarship is endowed by the institution then the scholarship cost must be included in the budget as a recruitment cost. It is obvious, therefore, that institutions should seek to capitalize on the fully funded scholarships available from outside sources. Government can be a full or co-sponsor through the ODASSS (Overseas Development Agency Scholarship Scheme) and ORS and ACU awards.[10] The availability of such scholarships raises the profile of the host institution and allows a greater freedom of choice in selecting students. The highest quality of student is attracted by such scholarships and they and their success add to the reputation of the institution. Chevening scholarships are funded by government and available in many countries.[11] Usually, they provide full funding for the student but can specify particular subject areas, such as social sciences. Any institution of higher education committed to successful international recruitment should consider working with these scholarship schemes and even adapting them for their own purposes. When an institution is focusing on a particular country, it may be possible to discuss co-funding of Chevening with the British Embassy or the British Council.

This co-funding can also be extended to include commercial partners. In this way, institutions may also work directly with commercial partners to create scholarships directed at certain courses or professions. A multinational civil engineering company may provide a scholarship for construction management for the nationals of a country where it intends to extend its workforce or its sales. Where there is a tradition of fundraising or private donations to an institution, these, too, can be directed towards scholarship schemes. Close liaison with the office responsible for fundraising is essential if scholarships for international students are to become part of this donation distribution. The communication and networking within the institution are important here, and this is stressed again in the second half of this chapter. Institutions of the age and reputation of Oxford and Cambridge have access to the type of endowment funding that allows scholarships to be provided on need to allow access entirely on merit. Other institutions are less fortunate in their funding and are unable to support some of the best qualified international students. Institutions at all levels, however, can investigate the possibility of establishing scholarships, either by fundraising, or by alumni approaches, or by deciding to pump-prime certain international activities with income from other sources. This is a decision that can prove very effective as a short-term measure and depends on discussion within the individual institutions.

Directing the scholarship

Scholarships can be given for specific courses, for identified countries, for particular categories of student or for special sponsors or special occasions. If a new course is to be launched, the cost of one or two part-scholarships may not exceed the cost of placing a series of advertisements, and may be of much longer lasting significance for the fortunate recipients. Scholarship posters displayed in carefully selected overseas institutions can provide more mutually pleasing results than can be obtained from some newspaper advertisements or blanket mail shots. There are times, too, when a particular country can be identified as a focus for marketing – perhaps to raise the profile somewhere where the market share is falling, or to assist in gaining a reputation in a country with little experience of UK education. On these occasions, a widely advertised scholarship (and, of course, the more generous the scholarship the more it is promulgated) can do a great deal to stimulate interest and encourage enquiry and application. In this way, the institution is being helped to gain the critical mass of student registrations and alumni, which ensures that it will be sufficiently known in that country to encourage further applications.

The definition of 'critical mass' is probably like that of wealth – 'more than we currently have'! It does seem, however, that once about 30 students from one country are registered at one time, there is a greater likelihood of the institution being on the road to more certain success. Obviously, 30 students from Cyprus or Oman will have more significance than 30 from Brazil or China, since the impact on the former by the returning students will be much greater.

Since it is clear, too, that not all courses and all levels of study are as attractive as others in the overseas market, some scholarships may be directed to particular areas of shortfall within the institutional plan. If research students are a top priority and undergraduates are plentiful, then it would not be inappropriate to direct tuition fee scholarships to postgraduates. Similarly, if engineering is failing to meet targets and social sciences oversubscribed with applicants, the direction of the scholarship is obvious. This may be one good reason for locating scholarship distribution centrally in order that the overall strategic objectives of the institution can be delivered.

Awarding the scholarship

Once the scholarship tool is recognized, there may be a number of suggestions for its use. Special groups of students could include those identified as particularly intellectually able on arrival, those who perform exceptionally well on the programme, those who are most in financial need, those with a special status and those whose commitment or whose sponsor's commitment deserves recognition. Checking entry grades and deciding equivalencies, then making judgements, can be time-consuming and invidious. Awards given for on-course performance may be better identified as prizes. Means testing is a difficult and precise process which requires skilled handling to avoid embarrassment and error. Alumni can be categorized as having a special status, as can the children of alumni, and institutions can be imaginative in their offerings. They should, however, be aware that each claim will have to be validated by production of birth certificate or checking of degree lists. There is a good argument for recognizing loyalty to the institution or special financial commitment, such as when parents choose to place two or more children with the same institution or when husbands and wives undertake full-time programmes together. Again, the relationship would have to be documented and the institution will have to have prepared a response to the interpretation of 'brother' in some cultures and the discussion of what the 'spouse' relationship might mean!

This recognition of the role of the sponsor can be taken further by scholarships through volume registrations. Each institution will be in a position to decide what it will regard as volume for this purpose. Forty students on the summer school may be easier to acquire than four students on a PhD programme. If a sponsor can be encouraged to place a regular and significant number of students with an institution, that sponsor may well demand or invite scholarships in return. It goes without saying that any responsible institution will wish to insist on the right of rejection of any student but, if acceptable applicants are generated, then the sponsor may well wish to receive a fee reduction. Discounts, fee waivers and reductions, for reasons to be discussed later in the chapter, may create difficulties, and scholarships, at the discretion of the awarding institution, can be helpful to both students and sponsors. They go some way to achieving a level of recognition for the host institution. Scholarships may also be initiated for special reasons – perhaps for signing a link agreement, the celebration of a jubilee, the publication of shared research. All of these are positive reinforcements of valued relationships. The need for scholarships for the South East Asian economic crisis of 1998 is too immediate at the point of writing for objective evaluation to be offered here. In brief, the scholarships are being offered to evidence commitment, to provide real and necessary support to existing students, and to attempt to protect markets which are among the largest for UK educational exports. Each institution will, therefore, as must always be the case, analyse its own position with regard to these groups of students and sponsors and respond within the terms of its own strategic plan. If the values identified in earlier chapters apply, then this plan and consequent response will bring together both the pastoral and the commercial imperatives.

The size of the award

Once the decision on categories of scholarship to be awarded has been made, then the institution needs to be clear on the size of the award. Is it to be a partial tuition fee scholarship, a full tuition fee award or a total scholarship with tuition, subsistence and travel covered? The first of these is most common and acts as encouragement to the well-qualified student who may be receiving a number of offers from UK and overseas institutions. Partial scholarships, too, can be added together by the tenacious student to provide something approaching full cover. Partial scholarships are often awarded and distributed after registration. Full tuition fee scholarships need to be awarded well in advance of registration since students seeking these may well be dependent on them for study overseas and once the award has been made, they need to make preparations for departure. As a generalization, students seeking partial scholarships are probably committed to, and financially capable of, study abroad in any event. Complete comprehensive scholarships are rarely offered by UK institutions and, for reasons outlined above, would certainly need to be awarded well before arrival.

Benefits and dangers

Whatever the form or the amount of the scholarship, the institution will benefit from maximum publicity, both of the scholarship availability and of its award. Happy stories of delighted students accompanied by smiling photographs with senior members of the institution make good news for the British Council, overseas offices and agents. This is not a cynical response: it is a recognition that bad news and adverse publicity travel quickly and widely, while sane, regular stories of success, generosity or achievement are often forgotten or bypassed.

All of the foregoing can be seen as an endorsement of an active, imaginative and sensibly handled scholarship scheme. Government scholarships, in particular, are an indication of UK goodwill towards the recipient and a national wish to maintain good relationships with that particular country. Chevening scholars, especially, have returned home over a number of years to do credit to themselves, their country and the UK institutions in which they studied. The institutional scholarship, as with any marketing tactic, however, can generate adverse comment and can give rise to less favourable interpretation.

- Will the UK institutions continue to make financial offers which eventually beat down the full-cost fee to the detriment of the whole system?
- Will what is offered more cheaply be confused with what is objectively assessed as the better quality product?
- Will sponsors restrict proper student choice because they can maximize their budgets by allying themselves to one or two institutions?
- Is encouragement inducement, and what does inducement mean?
- How are the most outstanding students from countries who are receiving less world aid to compete in the scholarship stakes with students from countries which are economically or politically attractive?

These are fascinating questions which stimulate the whole debate on the validity of locating entrepreneurial activity within the public sector ethos. If undergraduate courses were cars, the provider would, within the conventions of honesty and decency, be encouraged to advertise and market aggressively in order to achieve the best results for the company. Badly made cars would reduce the possibility of repeat orders. Although an appropriate price would have been set, there would be no objection to special offers being launched. Undergraduate courses are not cars, however, and institutions have the difficult dual responsibility of ensuring volume of sales and making judgements on the quality of the 'buyer'. If, however, standards are maintained and only those with appropriate academic and linguistic standards are allowed to 'buy', is there any problem with creative marketing? If the true cost of international recruitment is evaluated by the institution and can be seen to cover its cost or even generate a surplus while maintaining quality, can any more be required?

Sharing the cost

In providing resources for the full international recruitment activity, the institution has to decide how costs and benefits are to be apportioned between the centre and the departments. In some of the private institutions, this may not present any need for discussion as

success may simply be recognized by individual bonus arrangements. Similarly, in the worst-case scenario, failure may result
in unemployment. The public sector has not traditionally viewed
institutional resourcing as a matter of immediate significance to the
individual's salary cheque. The less favourable climate of the 1980s
and 1990s, with its efficiency savings, performance indicators, reduced proportion of HEFC or FEFC funding and increased revenue
drive, may lead to a more robust discussion of the relationship
between institutional success and continued employment. This is
not the place to debate the meaning of 'education' or 'success' or to
rehearse the fundamental arguments on autonomy and tenure. It is
merely a statement that there is evidence for the fact that academic
quality and financial health are not mutually exclusive (neither, of
course, are they mutually dependent). The success of the institution
in international recruitment, as in other activities, is, therefore, to
the overall benefit of the departments and, consequently, to the
individual members of staff.

The extent to which this benefit is experienced can be the basis
for a transparent and equitable distribution of costs, risk and reward
among these three groups. The equation relies upon the fact that
international students bring income and necessitate expenditure.
Tuition fee income is generally held centrally and is one of the
income streams which form part of the disbursement to the cost
centres. Any formula for distribution in the case of international
students may include resourcing per full-time equivalent student
(FTE) and/or incentive payments. Such incentive payments are made
specifically to encourage all colleagues to work towards the registration of well-qualified full fee-paying students. The payments are not
normally paid to the individual but to the account that benefits the
professional work of that individual. Some schemes do, however,
allow direct payment to the individual. It goes without saying that
the costs related to such schemes, such as scholarships or commissions to agents, should be borne in proportion to the advantage
gained, and that depends on the accounting system within the institution. If the agent works to a central office, it may be sensible for
that office to manage the budget and hence the commission payments. On the other hand, full-cost recovery courses may include
the agent's commission in their own budget. Certain subject-specific
scholarships may be fully funded from a devolved departmental
budget, particularly if a new course is being launched. Other scholarships for institution-wide use may be funded centrally. Others
may carry matched funding, with the centre and the departments
concerned dividing the cost according to an agreed formula. Course
advertisements in learned journals may be resourced by the

department(s), while insertions in more generic publications may be financed from the centre. Again, co-funding is another possibility.

Something as fundamental to international recruitment as travel expenditure is one of the largest budget heads and there should be a clear understanding of whose budgets are to be involved. If a number of departments or sections send individuals to represent their academic speciality and pay for them out of departmental resourcing, there could be a wasteful amount of duplicated effort. Members of the institution should be ambassadors for that institution whenever they appear professionally and much can be achieved when proactive colleagues participate in indirect promotional activities at courses, conferences, at meetings and on secondment throughout the world. Such commitment is of immense value to the whole enterprise. The duplication to be avoided occurs if every department believes that it can only be represented in formalized international recruitment activities by a departmental presence. It may even be prepared to pay for that presence. If a central office exists, which is charged with the responsibility for coordinating recruitment activities, it seems reasonable that that office, perhaps advised by other senior colleagues, select teams of travellers who can represent the institution as a whole to the best effect. Working towards the position where trust exists between the centre and the departments is the topic of the next section.

Networking – communication

The creation of the strategic plan was considered in Chapter 2. As was mentioned then, any plan is ineffective if it is not owned by a large proportion of the members of the institution it serves. The idealist would wish for 100 per cent ownership; the realist, knowing the pressures and tensions in an academic life, would wish for the support and understanding of a majority of the community. Those charged with the responsibility of ensuring that the targets within the plan are met and exceeded need to market as successfully inside the institution as outside. This cannot be done, however, at the expense of maintaining regular and constant external communications. Both activities are essential for the achievement of corporate objectives.

Internal communication

If information is power, then communication must be collegiality and, in a pressured world, is probably one of the first victims of bad time management. If the head of the institution with the executive group intend the plan to succeed, the officer or office responsible for implementing it should be charged with giving a high priority to internal communications and intelligent use of management information. This is the less 'glamorous' aspect of international recruitment but any who underrate it do so at their peril.

Making the most of the information

Application data is full of information that can be utilized to advantage.

- Which institutions do the applicants come from?
- What qualifications are presented and regularly rejected – would it be possible to establish a bridging course to facilitate entry for students holding those qualifications?
- Who are the sponsors and who provides the references?
- How did the applicants hear of the institution – was it through the exhibitions, alumni, advertisements, teachers, or the website?
- How many enquiries turn into applications and how many applications receive offers?
- How many of those holding offers register as students?
- Which institutions do applicants accept in preference to your own?
- What is the institutional wastage rate – is this reflected across all departments or more acute in some than others?
- Which qualifications from which overseas institutions are evidence of highly successful students?
- Which students from which international institutions write outstanding PhDs or which perform well at A Level?
- Which sponsors regularly send students and which send them sporadically?
- Which students hold prestigious scholarships – did they or their sponsors make the choice of institution?
- How many students studied in the host country before applying to the institution – would recruitment of international students be more effective and economical in London language schools and independent schools across the UK than in global travel?

In most institutions, most of this data exists, as indeed does much, much more. Working to increase recruitment without knowing the answers to most of these questions is like playing rounders in a blindfold! It becomes impossible to hit the ball squarely or field adequately. There should be office systems that can assimilate this information so that it can be provided in readable form to all those who need to understand it. The provision of all of this, particularly in terms of staff time, is an indirect cost on the international fee. Time spent in gaining this information and then putting it to good use is not wasted. Time spent on simply acquiring the information is dead time. The information needs to be worked on and digested so that once available and debated it can form a firm foundation for future planning. There are a number of examples that can make this point. Data reveals a high rate of rejection by UK institutions of Kenyan undergraduate applicants. This information can be shared with admission tutors and a discussion can take place on the reasons for it. It transpires that the majority of Kenyans applying now do so with KCSE. Most departments will not accept this for direct entry. It may be possible, therefore, to establish a one-year foundation course or to refer such candidates to local schools and colleges where accelerated A Levels and foundation courses are offered. Another set of data reveals that a certain Ministry had sponsored postgraduate students in the department of X for three consecutive years and then failed to send any further students. Discussion with the supervisors concerned indicates that two students had experienced difficulties with off-campus housing and language improvement and had sought extensions to complete their programmes. Correspondence with the Ministry followed up by a visit and the provision of figures showing the excellent completion rate of the department as a whole led to a re-establishment of good relations. Perhaps the students in question had refused the accommodation which was provided, perhaps they had absented themselves from the free in-sessional English language courses offered. Constructive dialogue with the sponsor could not only remedy the position but also lead to a more positive relationship for the future.

Sharing information

It can be seen from the foregoing that internal and external communications often overlap and the principles to be applied are those of transparency of decision making and spending, inclusivity of colleagues and sharing of information gained. The office that drives recruitment is likely to be in receipt of a large amount of valuable information. *Marketing News*, country surveys, sponsors' comments, overseas reports, all come into or are produced by the centre for international recruitment. Their value cannot be properly exploited by the small group of colleagues in that office but should be shared by all appropriate and interested colleagues through properly digested or edited synopses. Everyone likely to be involved with, for example, Turkish postgraduates will be interested in the changing role of YÖK, while all colleagues involved with Thai students in 1998 will appreciate information on British government and institutional provision made available for them. In large institutions it would be counterproductive to expect every academic department to deal with general issues such as accommodation, scholarships or qualification equivalence. It would be equally unacceptable to restrict information on these issues to one small office. Communication is time-consuming, labour-intensive (although much less so with email distribution lists), and easily overlooked, but the long-term effect of internal distribution of information is difficult to overestimate.

Communication is not simply a matter of duplicating all management information without thought as to direction or application. UCAS statistics on international offers made are of little use to a department without a comparative figure for the same time in the previous year or without the national application rate for comparator institutions. Can the department be helped with the conclusions to be drawn from these statistics? Is additional effort required, or is the position the best that can be achieved in the present circumstances? Is remedial action being recommended and assistance offered with it?

Passing on good practice

It is often necessary to respond to external invitations or demands as a matter of urgency and the overriding consideration then must be to take the decision with the colleagues empowered to ratify it and then to communicate it to the external organization. If the decision will have an effect on, or interest for, others within the institution, the next consideration should be to inform them of it. When scholarships are agreed, when deals are brokered, when relationships are signed off, it is necessary to inform those concerned with the financial and organizational implications. Similarly, when a department has recommended a special arrangement which has been agreed and concluded, such as twinning with or advanced standing for an institution overseas, then this information available to the central office should be published within the institution. Not only can one successful venture inspire others but all colleagues likely to be involved in travel to or negotiations with the institution need to be familiar with the whole picture. Examples of good practice within one area can also be made generally available. If one admissions tutor has created a very apt and well-worded letter to potential students, or unearthed a particularly successful source of funding, then this can be shared through a central office which can produce manuals of good practice and information available to all. Such manuals should include a list of international scholarships made available through the institution and at least an institutional protocol on dealing with international undergraduate admissions. In the best of all possible worlds such sharing of information will be reciprocal and departments will also inform the centre of interesting developments and opportunities.

Increasing participation

International travel can appear as an exciting and glamorous perk – this is generally only the perception, however, of those who have not been involved! Nevertheless, because of this perception every effort should be made to announce the dates of visits, venues to be included and the names and departments of participants well in advance. It should also be clear as to the rationale for the selection of international travellers. It is helpful, too, if the number of those experienced in such travel increases annually. This ensures that a small group and their departmental colleagues is not overextended by frequent absences, that the pool is enriched by the skills and strengths of new colleagues every year and that as large a proportion as possible of those with international interests and appropriate abilities is included. It is not an exclusive club with obscure membership criteria but a representative and growing cohort of academics and support staff from as many sections as possible. Specific issues on funding have already been considered but, in the main, all those travelling on the centrally held international budget should have broadly the same set of conditions, briefings and institutional ambassadorial responsibilities.

International recruitment of full fee-paying students is only one factor in the internationalization of the institution. Important or even critical as it is, as has been discussed in the introductory chapter, it is not the whole of the solution or the operation. Any office charged with international recruitment must, therefore, be aware of the value of, and indeed the existence of, a wealth of links and relationships, formal or informal, which the vast majority of academic colleagues will have developed with all parts of the world. A database on these links can provide the real picture of international activity as opposed to the more narrow one of students registered. It should be known, too, that those responsible for recruitment also have a genuine interest in non-recruitment specific international collaboration. Time, energy, support and sometimes resourcing can be offered to assist this collaboration which is of real academic value and satisfaction, even if the short-term financial dividend of recruitment is not obvious. In addition, the existence of thriving and successful links and achievements helps to round out the picture of activity for the institution as a whole.

Circulating information

It is unlikely that more than two colleagues will regularly travel together to any one country and yet the knowledge they gain, the impressions they receive and the contacts they make during that brief sojourn may well be of value to many, many departments. The need to prepare reports on return is, therefore, not only one of accountability but also of necessity in marketing terms. If the many departments who will be approached by good Mexican postgraduate students are to respond sensibly and positively, it is helpful if the views and recommendations of those with Mexican experience and insights have been made available. A good committee system can do this, but it can also be assisted by user friendly and expedient communication from the central office. In another example, UCAS admission officers are normally inundated by applications from home and overseas. If information has been gathered about particular schools during a visit, if contacts have been established, interest heightened and literature left, then the necessary follow-up on return home would be a dissemination of this information to these admission officers.

Whoever is responsible for international student activity could decide that many of these objectives can be met by the circulation of an internal newsletter at regular intervals. It is obvious that nothing commercially sensitive can appear, even in an internal publication, but a great deal of information can be provided on the recruitment environment, on travel, scholarships, available funding, new developments with regard to qualifications and general institutional thinking and direction. With the current information overload and pressures on time, it is often found that the briefer and clearer the documentation, the more favourable the response! This is another area in which electronic communication is often gratefully received.

Empowering colleagues

Every attempt should also be made to extend judgement and decision making to the widest community and to encourage everyone to come forward with views and suggestions. If qualification equivalencies are available on a web page, the individual academic colleague can reach a judgement on most postgraduate applicants. In addition, he or she may feel that it would be helpful to contact a central office to flesh out the information with more details about the institution from which the applicant comes, or for past experience of this qualification or issues relating to that nationality. The institution may wish to ensure consistency by putting in a second layer of vetting but individuals can take the initiative in deciding on recommending offer or rejection. If they choose not to do so, the central office will generally be only too pleased to advise or make suggestions on how to seek advice. All of these principles support the existence of academic autonomy within the context of the institutional mission, which has itself been decided and articulated by the academic community.

Not all communication needs to be conducted across the whole institution or through the written medium. Individual sections or departments may have specific issues on which they would like information, assistance and support. International officers meeting with colleagues can provide data of particular use to them, can discuss problems which have arisen from there, can offer help in a particular country in which they would like to expand, and can generally encourage, explain and support. A group making real efforts to meet the institution's objective and genuinely interested in internationalization merits the maximum support available. A central office can assist in the creation of mailing lists, help devise publicity, encourage with scholarships, consider including one of the group on visits, explain institutional procedures and devise specifically tailored letters to students. There should be almost unlimited support for a group with enthusiasm and commitment. There are other departments where the need or ability to recruit international students is well ahead of the willingness to do so. In meeting with these colleagues, the institution's list of incentives, both financial and less obvious, can be explained. There can be a discussion, too, on help that can be proffered and benefits that can accrue, rather than recriminations. If the department is willing to work in one area, rather than another (either geographical or by level of qualification), then means may be found to allow them to succeed in the chosen area. If study abroad students are, for some reason, easier to assimilate than postgraduates, then help can be directed at that area. The prime consideration with these more 'reluctant' groups would be to ensure that they understand their responsibility to the institution and that the first international students registered with them are as trouble-free, culturally undemanding and academically excellent as can be attracted!

Training and development

There is room, too, in any communication strategy for workshops and training programmes. Communication is a two-way activity and no International Office should promulgate information if it is unprepared to receive, in its turn, comments, criticisms and feedback.

If students from a given source all prove to be inadequate, if an English language test is seen to be invalid or a score unsatisfactory, if an institutional GPA, once reliable, is now variable – all of these can be communicated to the central office. If that office is constantly reminding admission tutors of the need for effective response to enquiries and yet never responds to colleagues' queries, then it should be made aware of that weakness. In short, the central office is the part of the team able to dedicate time and resource to the international objective and, therefore, to gain some expertise. It is not the sole holder of all knowledge, nor the generator of all good ideas. Some of the most successful developments have arisen from departmental initiatives and the International Office in these cases can only offer every help in implementation and hope to share in the reflected glory!

Many misconceptions which hamper internationalization can be addressed and may even be reversed by training sessions. These training sessions are not always the role of the International Centre alone but may be shared by a staff training and development unit. Such sessions can be focused on any group of colleagues and relate to any appropriate topic. A session for 'gatekeepers' might include porters, security staff, those involved in residential provision or with financial transactions. This workshop could explore some of the cultural differences in the countries from which the students come and discuss the views that the students are likely to hold on support staff, washing facilities, traffic regulations and financial procedures. Other sessions for catering staff can include the discussion of the content and importance of halal food, the need for pork-free or beef-free menus for some visitors and the difficulty of labelling dishes with the subsequent need for an explanation of 'toad-in-the-hole' or 'cottage pie'. These sessions can reinforce the sense of community within the institution and, as well as being enjoyable and informative, can stress the importance of the quality of the students' whole experience and sense of welcome. Workshops can be directed at variations in study skills and teaching methods, at English language remediation or culturally driven approaches to laboratory and practical skills. The institution should not feel that it needs to provide such training entirely from its own resources. UKCOSA has a long tradition of excellence in such training[12] and can offer bespoke courses for an institutional need or a wide range of open access programmes. Other groups, such as the Birmingham-based Consortium of Care, or the DTI, also run a number of programmes, as does the British Council. Ensuring that such courses exist, distributing information about them widely, and offering funding to support attendance, are all part of the responsibility of the central office.

While communication can be seen as the key to success in many areas of institutional management, it has an even higher profile when related to international student issues. So much in this area is dynamic, difficult to access, hedged about with misinterpretation and misunderstanding, muddled by quasi-commercial and political constraints, distorted by anecdote, excited by rumour, yet so vital to institutional health and success, that transparency and inclusivity are even more essential.

External communication

Keeping in touch with applicants and alumni

The institution that believes in itself is likely to subscribe to the view that the more the world knows about it, the more the world will wish to become part of it, and the more of the world that is in contact with it, then the more of the world that will apply to register with it! This being the case, every opportunity should be taken to maximize contact with the world outside the institution. While international travel and meetings can be arduous, often the more demanding tasks are the preparatory and follow-up activities. Much of the success of these depends on the quality of management information as discussed above. It is wise when planning a visit to contact alumni, arrange a meeting with them and give a presentation on recent developments within the institution. If the past students are A Level scholars, schools and colleges have often found it enjoyable to invite parents as well. Similarly, postgraduates frequently bring their spouses to such gatherings. Alumni activities are inevitably happy and positive occasions and the warmth of the feeling for the alma mater is humbling. Some institutions offer special scholarships for alumni or other concessions to them when returning to the home institution. As has been reiterated in other sections of the book, successful and personable alumni are the institution's best ambassadors and contact should be maintained even for that reason alone. They are also, however, as members of the institution, a real part of its international community and events with them are worthwhile and almost always rewarding. The decision as to when such alumni become part of an institution's fundraising activities lies outside the scope of this chapter and within the brief of the institution's development campaign.

Alumni gatherings can be extended to include all students from that country to whom offers of academic places have been made. They then have the opportunity of hearing first-hand of the experience of studying overseas. Such meetings with prospective students should bond them more closely to the institution and provide them with detailed information and immediate responses to any questions worrying them. Similarly, when visits to schools are made, the provision of up-to-date information on the students at the school who are in the applications process and the offers or the conditions made to them, together with knowledge of past students from that school, is vital. Potential undergraduates quite frequently build up a tradition of following the university choice of the preceding year and a letter from a student currently studying happily at the UK institution may considerably influence the UCAS contingent presently applying. Students have a knack of identifying for one another what is really important to them and a glowing description of the Halls of Residence or the squash courts may be more significant in student selection than the department's Teaching Quality Assessment as printed in the prospectus! If the overseas visit includes an exhibition, the traveller will be meeting and counselling a large number of students. It is a decision for the institution as to whether all of these should be contacted on return or only a proportion of them. Many may want additional literature or information, some will simply appreciate a letter offering continuing contact. There is no one perfect system of follow-up. The only unbreakable rule seems to be that if a promise to do something has been made, then it should be honoured.

Often offers are made to students months before they have to leave home to study overseas. When the pleasure of the offer has subsided, then the international potential student can be haunted by doubts and uncertainties. If the data collection is good enough, the institution can write to all students holding offers in the period before arrival, providing information, reassurance, or simply contact. Many of these students will never have seen the institution selected for their study; some of them will never have visited the country. A letter addressed to them personally, giving assurance of a warm reception, must, even to the most sophisticated, seem to offer reassurance.

The virtuous circle

The recruitment activity is continuous and circular. So much of what can be described as communication will have been considered under welfare and also as part of marketing. The whole, if successful, can be seen as a virtuous circle, revolving to create a system in which knowledge gained helps the institution to understand and so to offer support.

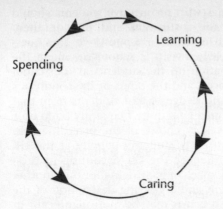

Figure 5.1   The virtuous circle

In this circle, these activities lead to income generation and consequent continued expenditure which allow in their turn more travel, greater exposure, more knowledge and increased welfare resourcing.

Valuing contacts

The institution, too, needs to be convinced of the need to network with the outside world. Every member of staff who travels can reflect the strengths and potential of the institution. Not everyone sees himself or herself as prepared for a recruitment role in its most limited interpretation but everyone within the institution must have a specialist ability and this can be used to effect. Physicists meeting others at a conference are, by their quality, promoting their own department and institution, albeit not in the same way as their colleagues running a presentation at the British Council Office.

The schools and language schools and specialist colleges in the host country should not be ignored as they are providing for and preparing a significant number of students wishing to pursue higher education in this country. If schools liaison activities do not have the capacity or the knowledge to interact with these institutions then the International Centre can include them in its brief. In country school visits, school dialogue and mail shots can be an important part of international marketing but, once again, the data has to be gathered and digested before these schools can be successfully identified. Similarly, large national organizations can often play a peripheral, yet important, role in overseas development. In the UK, for example, the Department of Trade and Industry, the Foreign and Commonwealth Office, Chambers of Commerce, all have information and connections which can be trawled. Every institution has a mix of local connections in the vicinity and the region which can be investigated.

- Sometimes the Member of Parliament sits on a Select Committee in the House or chairs a parliamentary international friendship group.
- Many MPs have a wide circle of international connections.
- Local businesses may be international or multinational in their sales or in their purchase of raw materials.
- The local hospital may have doctors on attachment from other countries.
- Conferences held in the institution may include overseas delegates.
- Local Rotary Clubs may have visits from overseas counterparts.
- Local government may be involved in town twinning or in regional activity overseas.
- Honorary graduates may have an international reputation or be part of an international circuit.

The number of encounters that a large educational institution has with the outside world is almost limitless and so the opportunities for international contact are immense. The effort required to learn about them, codify them, evaluate them and exploit them would be enormous but, if only a small proportion of these were successfully followed up, the international image of the institution, and thus its potential for recruitment, would be considerably enhanced.

Conclusion

If the institution has a will to see international activity as a valued part of its corporate strategy, it will need to resource it properly. This resourcing must include the ability to gather data which is vital to its marketing success and it must schedule time to evaluate the data and maximize its worth. Once the data has been so digested it can be opened up and shared with all parts of the institution, so that every member of it feels he or she not only has a commitment to the international agenda but also understands how to gain the detailed knowledge which allows him or her to play a significant role, whether by travelling overseas or offering a sympathetic reception at home.

Endnotes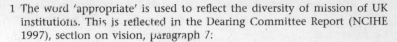

1 The word 'appropriate' is used to reflect the diversity of mission of UK institutions. This is reflected in the Dearing Committee Report (NCIHE 1997), section on vision, paragraph 7:

> The higher education sector will comprise a community of free-standing institutions dedicated to the creation of a learning society and the pursuit of excellence in their diverse missions. It will include institutions of world renown and it must be a conscious objective of national policy that the UK should continue to have such institutions. Other institutions will see their role as supporting regional or local needs. Some will see themselves as essentially research orientated; others will be predominately engaged in teaching. But all will be committed to scholarship and to excellence in the management of learning and teaching.

2 As at March 1998, these were subdivided as:

Higher education 146
Further education 63
Independent schools/tutorial colleges 36
ELT schools 36
Associate members 5

This shows a period of steady growth from the single-sector group which first subscribed to ECS in 1983.

3 *Marketing News*, produced regularly by ECS, had by September 1998 reached edition 51. Information is focused by country and divided into sections relating to:

- national developments;
- local education developments;
- competitor activity;
- recent and forthcoming events;
- miscellaneous.

4 The ECS, funded as a partnership by grant-in-aid from the British Council and the subscribing institutions, is managed by a Board comprising:

3 HE members (elected)
2 FE (elected)
1 private and school sector member (elected)
2 Vice-Chancellors (nominated by the CVCP)
3 senior British Council staff
Director ECS acts as the Secretary

The role of the Board of Directors

> is to set and approve the policy of ECS so as to ensure its financial viability and that it achieves the objectives and targets agreed in the Business Plan. The Board is not involved in the executive management

of ECS which is the responsibility of Director ECS, who is appointed by the British Council, on the advice of the Board.

(Education Counselling Service, Board of Directors, British Council, September 1998)

5 Event levies listed in 1998 start from £300 for the Cyprus Clearing Mission and range up to £3000 for the two-centre Japan British Education Exhibition.

6 The FCO Travel Advice website can be found on http:/www.fco.gov.uk/travel/default.asp. The introduction states:

FCO's Consular Division produces a range of material intended to advise and inform British citizens travelling abroad. This includes advice to help British travellers avoid trouble, especially threats to their personal safety arising from political unrest, lawlessness, violence, natural disasters, epidemics, anti-British demonstrations and aircraft safety.

Examples of advice were, in August 1998:

• Iraq – British nationals should not attempt to visit Iraq.
• Vietnam – Travel in parts of Vietnam can be hazardous and, in some areas, restricted.
• Kuwait – Care should be taken when using beaches and picnic spots. Even where officially cleared there is still a danger from unexploded ordinance.

7 It is a useful general guideline that if the British Embassy flies its staff out of country for medical treatment then the medical facilities in-country are less than satisfactory.

8 The British Airways website (http:/www.british-airways.com) includes Travel Clinics. They offer 'sound advice on keeping healthy while abroad.' Advice is given on immunization: 'Yellow Fever – A single injection provides protection against yellow fever for ten years. An International Certificate of Vaccination against Yellow Fever is valid ten days after the injection and is a mandatory request for entry into certain countries', but not on specific country requirements.

9 Most HE institutions use tuition fee band definitions which apply to full-time award-bearing courses as follows:

Band 1 Courses which do not involve significant laboratory, workshop or studio activity
Band 2 Laboratory-based courses or any other courses where costs are likely to be on a similar scale
Band 3 Clinical stage of medicine

English studies or law would probably be in Band 1 (the lowest tuition fee) while music and architecture could be in Band 2.

10 These refer to scholarships offered through the Department for International Development, to the Overseas Research Students Scheme and to the Association of Commonwealth Universities programme.

11 Chevening Scholarships are named after the official country residence of the British Foreign Secretary.
12 UKCOSA has also collaborated with one British university to offer an MA programme in International Education which can be accessed in part through its accredited short course programme. More information on UKCOSA can be found in Chapters 1 and 4. The British Council is also establishing a scheme of professional development ultimately leading to accreditation.

6

THE WAY AHEAD

Introduction

Every year it seems that a greater number of students choose to travel overseas to study part or all of an award-bearing programme. The international student industry is a thriving and expanding one and yet there is no security as to how this multi-billion dollar business will develop. The only thing that can be stated with certainty is that the future is uncertain. The arrival of full fee-paying students in the host country for courses taught by the host institutions depends on the happy coincidence of a large number of variables – most of which lie outside the control of even the most diligent of institutional managers.

What follows can at best be a review of possibilities in the British context – every recruiting country will have a unique set of factors but all may recognize some of the following.

The variables

To achieve the results to which the institutions aspire in their plans it is not enough to represent an establishment of acknowledged academic excellence with sensitive and well-resourced support systems. It is not enough to market intelligently and to promote with commitment and enthusiasm. For these plans to succeed, the UK must be free from internal or external aggression – the miners' strike, the Northern Ireland experience and the Gulf War gas threats did much to discourage recruitment. In a similar vein outbreaks of violent crime in parts of the USA always boost the UK market share. The media is global and dramatic scenes of localized unrest are quickly beamed around the world.

The UK too must be seen to value its own educational institutions and those who work in them. Low morale, reductions in spending, decline in facilities, discontented home students, demotivated support staff are all factors which could become apparent – especially when in many other countries the status of teacher and scholar is one of prestige and dignity. Again the media is quick to publicize stories of disappointment, decline and dissension which, taken out of context, can portray a system which is less than robust. The British do not have a strong sense of the sacred and higher education is, by its very nature, iconoclastic. The very liberality and seeking after truth which marks an educational system of excellence can generate that irreverence and self-deprecation which leads the British to comment ironically upon and criticize some of their finest institutions. In addition, the government must continue to require the public sector institutions to charge a differential fee for home and European Union (HEU) and international students. If the home student fee were eventually increased to match the full-cost fee and such students required to meet their own fees, then the financial imperative to recruit international students would be removed. In the same way, institutional budgets and marketing strategy could be significantly affected by the extension of membership of the European Union. Recently, Finland and Sweden were introduced to the Union with the consequent loss of fee income to the UK, and the need for these students to compete for 'home' places. Norway has, for the present, remained outside the block but Cyprus and Turkey are pressing for entry. If institutions are looking for fee income and these countries, together with others in Eastern Europe, are eventually admitted, more and more attention will be focused on those outside the Union as a source for international fee-paying students. Those institutions whose agendas are truly international will welcome the free movement of students from the EU family, while others may only be prepared to accept them as paying guests.

The sending countries must remain at peace with the UK and free of embargo or restriction. Iraqi students are no longer able to study here and UN embargoes on India and Pakistan over recent nuclear testing could affect their ability to contract with the UK. Similarly, the countries from which our students come must be free from currency restrictions, exchange control regulation impediments and visa inhibitions. Economic or natural disasters or political upheaval all destabilize an international marketing strategy.

Selective scenarios ∎

Exponential leaps forward in information technology and in our awareness of one world and global citizenship have also created a series of visions of the future, any or all of which could change the nature of national or international education.

Collaboration and development

At one stage it was believed that in order to gain a qualification from a UK institution, the entire period of study had to be spent in that institution in the UK. Many sponsors now see this as the 'luxury' model. It may continue to exist for those who wish and can afford to be exposed to a cultural experience as well as an international training. What is 'better' is perhaps not in question but rather what is feasible. The developing countries are moving steadily towards a position where, for the majority of their citizens, further education and undergraduate courses can be delivered in the main by their own institutions. Skills courses, training programmes, staff development, consultancy and collaboration still remain as options for host institutions, as do niche marketing opportunities. This means that those institutions who have, for more than a decade, welcomed large numbers of students onto their regular courses may now be looking to maintain such contacts with other more flexible delivery mechanisms. The patterns of franchise, twinning and offshore delivery have been considered in an earlier chapter. With more effective international travel facilities, better understanding of cross-cultural issues, greatly enhanced availability of information through the net, such schemes are easier to establish and control. With a change in attitude within the UK institutions, they will be easier to promote. With too great an appetite for commercial returns on either side, they will be easy to abuse. The responsibility for the establishment and the monitoring of such schemes is a heavy one. For the sake of proper control and accountability, any host institution involved should separate the quality control of such schemes from the section accountable for their financial success. The International Office and the Quality Audit Office will work with shared objectives but with a system of checks and balances that perpetually reminds the one of the long-term goal and the other of present realities.

Not only is the sub-degree and first degree market changing but also the postgraduate menu is being modified to suit customer need and capability. The research degree can be offered with joint supervision, intercalation and block placement. The host supervisor can travel to the student, the overseas supervisor can collaborate in the supervision or the student can attend the host institution to take advantage of certain facilities and strengths offered there which can be incorporated into study for an overseas award. We recognize the growing research strengths and specialist skills of other nations and their capability to be responsible for a portion of the final degree. We recognize the financial constraints of reputable national sponsors who need to disperse their scholarships to as many well-qualified applicants as possible. We recognize various cultural constraints such as those which do not allow women to remain unchaperoned overseas, necessitating limited periods of UK supervision if such women are to be allowed to succeed. We recognize the growing and proper aspirations of maturing overseas institutions to prove themselves capable of offering one part of a Taught Masters programme in collaboration with an overseas provider. All these modifications and movements can be seen as part of a transition to a condition where the overseas institutions have developed to a point of partnership rather than dependency.

Collaboration and mobility

Employers require global awareness. Internationalism has become the watchword and the industrialized nations have recognized the force of world economics, the effect of multinationals on national policy and the value of the mobility of labour. Institutions of quality have long recognized the worth of the qualifications awarded by overseas institutions – graduates from institutions all over the world find their degrees recognized and welcomed in the developed countries. There is now an opportunity, through this positive attitude of educationalists and employers and through the massive advances in IT, for students to earn qualifications through an accumulation of credits from other recognized institutions. For many years, the undergraduate study abroad programme, once called the JYA (Junior Year Abroad) has allowed and encouraged North American students to study in and gain credits from a host institution. This system is now extended to Japan, Korea, Taiwan, Latin America and Australia.

British students, other than those on language or area studies programmes, have not found it easy to join such exchange schemes and most of the international traffic is one-way and brings income to the UK. The position is changing. The European mobility schemes allow the institutions to encourage their students to spend a year or a semester under the ERASMUS or the SOCRATES programme. UK engineers found that they could study in the institutions across

Europe and be assessed in a second language. The experience and the skills gained considerably enriched their CVs and employment potential. UK institutions learned that it was possible to permit their students time away from their UK campus and possible to accept the marks or grades with which they returned. The opportunities for the future will be yet more exciting and challenging. Institutions of higher education have already begun to make world alliances with establishments of similar quality to create on each campus a node of a global university. Consortia like Universitas 21,[1] with participants in the UK and across the world, will work towards allowing students to move between sites and to accumulate credits from courses taught in a number of locations. It is not only the students who will benefit. Staff of all categories may view the whole as a confederation of like-minded systems with common objectives as to excellence in research, teaching, governance and professionalism and so may find mobility of employment within the UK. Such networks will encourage exchange of students and so eventually decrease the importance of the fee which the student brings and increase the sense of true internationalism through the world community of scholars.

The global university

It is a small step from such visions, already tentatively becoming reality, to the university which has no single physical location. Knowledge, through the electronic media, through satellite and the ever-expanding availability and cost reduction of the home workstation, need not be restricted to the location of an individual leading scholar or a cache of literature or journals. The virtual university[2] with its promise of global learning and constant accessibility has already been foreshadowed by the internet PhD and virtual schools and departments. There may be a time when an eminent researcher or teacher does not choose to spend his or her career in Oxford or Harvard, Singapore or the Sorbonne but works under the aegis of the British Aerospace or IBM University or their like. As the medieval student physically followed the wandering scholar before such scholars collected into a formal location, so the student of the future may follow intellectually a strand of argument across the ether. Over the millennium the principle may have come full circle.[3]

Many educational, social and pedagogic issues will need to be debated before this comes about, many of which will be of importance to the UK student as well as those overseas. Envisaging the education of the future is not within the scope of this study but it is relevant to note that the pace of change of content and delivery will be rapid, such that our existing views on provision for international students and reliance on the income they generate will be challenged. Indeed, the whole idea of the international student as differentiated from the home student may be inappropriate when the learning process and the qualification awarded for it are no longer nationally based. Futurologists have been wrong before and the professional life span of many of those today concerned with international students – their recruitment, education, care and commercial value – may well have ended before such shadows attain substance.

In the shorter term we can look to the income from international recruitment being reduced by the expansion of the European Union, the increase in demand for student exchange, the downturn of major world economies and the growth of provision in various overseas countries. Perhaps the most significant of all of these 'threats' would be a perceived and believed decline in the quality of UK plc. No system is without fault but constant antagonistic competition, weaknesses which remain unremedied, bad practice which has been allowed to succeed, greed which is unchallenged and low standards which are uncorrected prejudice not only the reputation of the individual institution to which they pertain, but the system as a whole. In the academic world where autonomy is treasured and intellectual diversity encouraged, there must yet be a recognition that 'I am my brother's keeper.'

The converse is also true and in many ways UK plc has never been in a stronger position to take advantage of opportunity. Assessments, audits, codes and transparency are all making clear the strength of the UK institutions at school, college and university level. The excellence of what can be offered is obvious and, after a generation of wider international participation, the advantages and pleasures of so doing are more apparent. Members of staff may today enrich their teaching experience by relating to well-qualified students of all nationalities. They may travel across the world to counsel and interview them; they may spend time in another continent teaching and examining them. The income created by their fees allows better services, better facilities, more imaginative and focused marketing. The level of care which the international student enjoys today has never been higher. Countries once dependent on aid and scholarship now have a small but expanding middle class with aspirations for their children. Students from Vietnam, Myanmar, China and Russia are not only studying in schools in the UK but proving their ability to progress through the higher education system. Institutions can disburse the income generated from successful volume recruitment in the more affluent countries in scholarship schemes to assist the able but less advantaged student. China, parts of Africa and countries suffering intermittent difficulties can receive institutional or national scholarships. In addition to all of this, the rewards of including the gifted student from another culture have become obvious. From the food the institution serves to the customs which it recognizes, from the case studies that it incorporates in its teaching to the values that it incorporates in its daily life, UK plc has been enriched. Of such enrichment, fee generation is but a small component.

Conclusion

1980 marked not only a change in the way that non-EU international students paid for their education in the UK but also the birth of a new profession. International students had to be sought and wooed in the face of competition for their favours from competitors in the US, Canada, Australia, New Zealand, Germany, France and, latterly, regional centres in Asia. A private enterprise culture had to be engendered and accommodated within the public sector ethos. The tensions between tradition and pragmatism, quality and flexibility, had to be resolved to the satisfaction of each individual institution. The participation of these students was no longer seen as a privilege for them, but a necessity for the institution seeking them. Every member of that institution had to become aware of the rewards of recruitment successfully undertaken, and teaching and care successfully delivered. Management had to recognize that certain additional skills were needed, had to identify the scope and shape of the enterprise, had to allocate resources to the endeavour and appoint colleagues to undertake these activities. Perceptions changed and the change in terminology reflected the change in attitude. Those who were in the 1970s described as **foreign** students were the **overseas** students of the 1980s and the **international** students of the present decade. Through the necessity imposed by government has come a new set of values and skills which in the majority of cases have added to the totality of the UK education dimension.

Endnotes

1 Universitas 21 was established in March 1997 as an international association of major research-intensive universities designed to enrich the educational research and scholarly functions of the member institutions, to strengthen their capacity to operate internationally and to enhance their international recognition and standing. Members now include:

University of New South Wales	
University of Queensland	Australia
University of Melbourne	
McGill University	
University of British Columbia	Canada
University of Toronto	
Fudan University	China
Peking University	
University of Hong Kong	Hong Kong
University of Auckland	New Zealand
National University of Singapore	Singapore
University of Birmingham	
University of Nottingham	United Kingdom
University of Glasgow	
University of Edinburgh	
University of Michigan	USA

Several others are in the process of joining.

2 There is much discussion on the potential of the virtual campus. One example of the views expressed states:

> The search for the international campus is, of course, vastly influenced by developments in the use of information technology. The Internet and the World Wide Web are opening up tremendous learning opportunities, as courses become available on-line. The notion of a university as a physical entity is already being questioned.'

Maeve Sherlock and the late Steve Sharples (1998) then went on to question whether this will indeed be the case. 'Education is intrinsically about people and relationships, not machines.'

There is a question of accessibility of facilities. 'While there are some thirty million people which have access to that Internet, another three billion or so do not.'

3 The definition of education has been a subject for philosophers and educationalists from Plato to Dearing. Some believe that Robbins made the best attempt at articulating the purpose of higher education. Maybe the most articulate and memorable, but certainly not that which carries the greatest consensus, was stated in 1873 by Newman and then echoed in the Dearing Report some 115 years later. Newman believed that higher education should aim at:

> raising the intellectual tone of society, at cultivating the public mind, at purifying the national task, at supplying true principles to popular enthusiasm and fixed aims to popular aspirations, at giving enlargement and sobriety to the ideas of the age, at facilitating the exercise of political power, and refining the intercourse of private life.
>
> (Newman 1905: 133)

Dearing quotes John Masefield (in his address to the University of Sheffield, 1946) as describing institutions of higher education as:

a place where those who hate ignorance may strive to know; where those who perceive truth may strive to make others see; where seekers and learners alike, banded together in that search for knowledge, will honour thought in all its finer ways, will welcome thinkers in distress or in exile, will uphold ever the dignity of thought and learning and will exact standards in these things.

(NCIHE 1997)

USEFUL CONTACTS

British Airways
Travel Clinic
Website address: http:/www.british-airways.com

British Council
Education Counselling Service
Bridgewater House
58 Whitworth Street
Manchester
M1 6BB
Tel: 0161 957 7000

British Council
Information Centre
10 Spring Gardens
London
SW1A 2BN
Tel: 0161 957 7163

Committee of Vice-Chancellors and Principals (CVCP)
Woburn House
20 Tavistock Square
London
WC1H 9HQ
Tel: 0171 419 4111

Department of Trade and Industry
Education and Training Sector Group
Kingsgate House
66–74 Victoria Street
London
SW1E 6SW
Tel: 0171 215 5000

Foreign and Commonwealth Office
Website address: http:/www.fco.gov.uk/travel/default.asp

Hospitality for Overseas Students Trust (HOST)
18 Northumberland Avenue
London
WC2 5BJ

Quality Assurance Agency
Southgate House
Southgate Street
Gloucester
GL1 1UB
Tel: 01452 557 000

United Kingdom Council for Overseas Student Affairs
    (UKCOSA: for International Education)
9–17 St Albans Place
London
N1 0NX
Tel: 0171 226 3762

UK NARIC
c/o ECCTIS
Oriel House
Oriel Road
Cheltenham
GL50 1XP
Tel: 01242 260010

BIBLIOGRAPHY

Allen, Michael (ed.) (1988) *The Goals of Universities*. Milton Keynes. SRHE and Open University Press.

Armytage, W.H.G. (1955) *Civic Universities, Aspects of a British Tradition*. London: Ernest Benn.

British Council (1979) *Director General's Report*, 4 December.

British Council (1980) *Board Minutes*, 1 April.

British Council (1981) *Report of Ditchley Park Conference*, 3 February.

British Council (1982) *Board Minutes*, 10 June.

British Council (1983a) *A Policy for Overseas Students*, Annex B, Board Minutes, August.

British Council (1983b) *Board Minutes*, 1 February.

British Council (1984) *Board Minutes*, 3 April.

British Council (1985a) *Board Minutes*, 2 April.

British Council (1985b) *Board Minutes*, 1 October.

British Council (1995) *Educating Gita: The £1bn Business Opportunity*. London: British Council.

British Council (1997a) *Pakistan Market Plan: The Promotion of UK Education and Training Services*. Manchester: British Council.

British Council (1997b) *The Promotion of UK Education and Training Services in Pakistan, Market Report*. Manchester: British Council.

British Council (1998) *ECS Programme of Events 1998/1999*. Manchester: British Council.

British Council (1998) *Education Counselling Service. The Board of Directors*. Manchester: British Council.

British Council (1998) *Some Facts and Figures 1996/97*. London: British Council.

British Council (various dates) *Marketing News*. Manchester: British Council.

Chandler, A. (1989) *Obligation or Opportunity: Foreign Student Policy in Six Major Receiving Countries*. New York: Institute of International Education.

Childs, W.M. (1936) *The Justification of Universities*. Manchester: J.M. Dent and Sons.

Cobban, A.B. (1975) *The Medieval Universities – Their Development and Organisation*. London: Methuen.

Committee of Vice Chancellors and Principals (CVCP) (1998) *HE Briefing Service: International Students in UK Higher Education* (July). London: CVCP.

CUA/APA (1989) Study Group Report *Strategic Choice: Corporate Strategies for Change in Higher Education*. Conference of University Administrators/ Association of Polytechnic Administrators.

Eggins, H. (ed.) (1988) *Restructuring Higher Education*. Milton Keynes: SRHE and Open University Press.

Fisher, H.A.L. (1936) *A History of Europe*. London: Edward Arnold.

Flexner, A. (1930) *Universities American, English, German*. Oxford: Oxford University Press.

Greenaway, D. and Tuck. J. (1995) *Economic Impact of International Students in UK Higher Education*. London: CVCP.

Higher Education Quality Council (1996) *Code of Practice for Overseas Collaboration Provision in Higher Education*, 2nd edn. London: HEQC.

Jarratt, A. and Sizer, J. (1987) *Institutional Responses to Financial Reductions within the University Sector*. London: DES.

Journal of International Education (various dates) 1(1, 2); 2(1); Supplementary Issue January 1991.

Kinnell, M. (1988) Marketing courses to overseas students: a case study of two universities, in H. Eggins (ed.), *Restructuring Higher Education*. Milton Keynes: SRHE and Open University Press.

Kogan, M. and D. (1983) *The Attack on Higher Education*. London: Kogan Page.

Lauder, D. (1998) Telephone interview, April 1998.

Mansbridge, A. (1922) *The Older Universities of England*. London: Longmans Green.

Masefield, J. (1946) Address to the University of Sheffield.

Moodie, G.E. (ed.) (1986) *Standards and Criteria in Higher Education*. Milton Keynes: SRHE/Open University Press.

NCIHE (National Committee of Inquiry into Higher Education) (1997) *Higher Education in the Learning Society* (The Dearing Report). London: NCIHE.

Newman, J.H. (1905) The idea of a university, in *Lectures*. London: Longmans, Green and Co. (first published 1873).

Overseas Student Trust (1982) *The Next Steps: Overseas Student Policy into the 1990s*. London: Overseas Student Trust.

Peat Marwick (1986) *Current Issues in Public Sector Management*. London: Peat Marwick.

Rashdall, H. (1936) *The Universities of Europe in the Middle Ages*. Oxford: Oxford Clarendon Press.

Robbins, Lord (1963) *Higher Education Report*, Cmnd 2154. London: HMSO.

Scott, P. (1998) *The Globalization of Higher Education*. Buckingham: Open University Press.

Sharples, S. (1997) *Contrasting Approaches to International Education: Views from Around the World*. London: UKCOSA.

Sherlock, M. and Sharples, S. (1998) In search of the international campus. *Journal of International Education*, Spring, 9(1).

Shinn, C.H. (1983) *The history of the development of the University Grants Committee*. PhD thesis, University of Nottingham.

Shinn, C.H. (1986) *Paying the Piper: The Development of the University Grants Committee*. Lewes: Falmer.

Silver, H. and P. (1986) The escaping answer, in G.E. Moodie (ed.), *Standards and Criteria in Higher Education*. Milton Keynes: SRHE/Open University Press.

Simmons, J. (1959) New University. Unpublished PhD thesis, University of Nottingham.

Stephens, Michael D. (ed.) (1989) *Universities, Education and the National Economy*. London: Routledge.

Taggart, S. (1998) Britain's top 100 Universities, *Financial Times Guide*, 29 April.

Times Higher Education Supplement (1979) Interview with Dr Rhodes Boyson, 16 November.

Times Higher Education Supplement (1998) Opinion, 2 January.

Tysome, T. (1998) Overseas controls. *Times Higher Education Supplement*, 23 January.

UKCOSA (1997) *International Students in the UK: The Recent Literature*. London: UKCOSA.

University of Nottingham (1997) *Research Student and Supervisors: A Guide 1997/98*. Nottingham: University of Nottingham.

Vale, B. (1990) Overseas students: the current state of the game. *Journal of International Education*, 1(1).

Warner, D. (1990) The new professionals (first editorial). *Journal of International Education*, 1(1).

INDEX

MANAGING STUDENTS

John M. Gledhill

Managing Students guides managers and administrators through the complexities which can lurk within the apparently straightforward tasks of student administration. It ranges from the big issues of judicial review to the seemingly trivial question of why examination desks move. It explores how managers can balance the needs of the students with those of the institution; how they can make sure they have thought of all the things that can go wrong; and how they can ensure that academics and students understand why things have to be done a certain way. It provides clear and helpful guidance on how to approach the incredibly varied tasks of student administration; on, for instance: how disabled students take examinations; whether the courts can overturn examination results; what you can write in references; the many ways in which students can cheat; and the rationale behind degree ceremonies.

Managing Students is both an accessible guide to the relevant issues and a practical, 'hands on' professional text for all those involved in student administration.

Contents
Introduction – Recruitment, retention and aftercare – Course construction and module choice – Examinations – Awards ceremonies and certificates – Discipline – Records and transcripts – Financial and legal obligations – Confidentiality, data protection, references – Afterword: the future – References – Index.

160pp   0 335 20256 X   (Paperback)   0 335 20257 8 (Hardback)

MANAGING QUALITY AND STANDARDS
Colleen Liston

Quality management, the application of standards and client service are as important in post-secondary education as they are in any other business or public service activity. Colleen Liston provides a practical, common sense approach to using procedures and information to demonstrate improved performance and to account for outcomes.

She explores questions such as:

- what is the current state of play on the assessment of quality and standards in universities and colleges?
- how can the 'quality movement' be successfully adapted to post-secondary education?
- how can colleges and universities take control of their own quality and standards: what are the principles and guidelines?

Managing Quality and Standards confronts both the quality jargon and the cynicism of many academics about the 'quality police'. It is full of practical examples and guidelines for action and will be very useful to managers in universities and colleges worldwide.

Contents
Introduction: terms, principles and practices – Historical aspects of the quality debate – Quality assurance in post-secondary education: an international overview – Quality improvement in education environments – Linking quality management to planning – Benchmarking and best practice – Models to consider – Pulling the threads together – Appendix: Definition of terms – Notes – Bibliography – Index.

208pp   0 335 20208 X   (Paperback)   0 335 20209 8 (Hardback)

THE GLOBALIZATION OF HIGHER EDUCATION

Peter Scott

This book describes and analyses the links between the growth of mass higher education systems and the radical processes of globilization which include not only round-the-clock, round-the-globe markets and new information technologies but revolutionary conceptions of time and space. Higher education is implicated as creator, interpreter and sufferer of these trends. *The Globalization of Higher Education* attempts to make sense of the connections between the expansion (and diversification) of higher education – including the increasing emphasis on international collaboration and the recruitment of international students – and the development of global politics, markets and culture. It offers a variety of perspectives, including those of national policies (from the UK, Europe and South Africa), of the European Union, of the Commonwealth, and of UNESCO.

This is a first, significant attempt to put the transformation of higher education within the more general context of globalization.

Contents
Preface – Contemporary transformations of time and space – Internationalizing British higher education: students and institutions – Internationalizing British higher education: policy perspectives – Internationalization in Europe – Internationalization in South Africa – A commonwealth perspective on the globalization of higher education – The role of the European Union in the internationalization of higher education – Globalization and concurrent challenges for higher education – Massification, internationalization and globalization – Index – The Society for Research into Higher Education.

144pp   0 335 20244 6   (Paperback)   0 335 20245 4 (Hardback)